QUICK BRAINSTORMING ACTIVITIES FOR BUSY MANAGERS

QUICK BRAINSTORMING ACTIVITIES FOR BUSY MANAGERS

50 Exercises to Spark Your Team's Creativity and Get Results Fast

Brian Cole Miller

American Management Association

New York • Atlanta • Brussels • Chicago • Mexico City • San Francisco
Shanghai • Tokyo • Toronto • Washington, D. C.

This publication is designed to provide accurate and authoritative information in regard to the subject matter covered. It is sold with the understanding that the publisher is not engaged in rendering legal, accounting, or other professional service. If legal advice or other expert assistance is required, the services of a competent professional person should be sought.

Library of Congress Cataloging-in-Publication Data

Miller, Brian Cole
  Quick brainstorming activities for busy managers : 50 exercises to spark your team's creativity and get results fast / Brian Cole Miller.
     p. cm.
  Includes bibliographical references and index.
  ISBN-13: 978-0-8144-1792-8
  ISBN-10: 0-8144-1792-2
  1. Creative ability in business. 2. Teams in the workplace. I. Title.
  HD53.M548 2012
  658.4'022—dc23

                                                                2011025999

About AMA
American Management Association (www.amanet.org) is a world leader in talent development, advancing the skills of individuals to drive business success. Our mission is to support the goals of individuals and organizations through a complete range of products and services, including classroom and virtual seminars, webcasts, webinars, podcasts, conferences, corporate and government solutions, business books, and research. AMA's approach to improving performance combines experiential learning—learning through doing—with opportunities for ongoing professional growth at every step of one's career journey.

Printing number

10 9 8 7 6 5 4 3 2 1

CONTENTS

ACKNOWLEDGMENTS

Thank you to the many friends and colleagues who gave me encouragement for this book, as well as some great activities. This includes you Jim Fograscher, Terry Hildebrandt, Tony Lipscomb, Roshan Massey, Alejandro Rodriguez, Leigh Ann Rogers, and Scott Shaffer.

Special thank you to Mark Hansen of "sparkspace" in Columbus, Ohio. Your work in getting folks creative is wonderful. Thanks for sharing your techniques so freely.

Another special thank you to Michael Wilkinson of Leadership Strategies in Atlanta. Your approach to putting structure and discipline to facilitation is fantastic. Thanks for letting me use some of the brainstorming and prioritizing activities you developed.

Thank you Christina Parisi and your colleagues at AMACOM for keeping me on track, and for being patient with me when I dragged my feet.

Thank you Debbie Posner, who cleaned up my writing so well, it actually makes sense to readers now, and thanks to Mike Sivilli, who shepherded the manuscript through to finished product.

Thank you Ed Buns for the great artwork. A picture is worth 1,000 words, and your work helped save me a lot of 1,000-words's.

Thank you Martin and David for letting me do much of my creative work at your lovely cottage in Ireland. Makes me want to write another book just so I can go back!

Thank you family—Heidee, Benjamin, Logan, Roger, Theresa, and Tina—for your ongoing support as I wrote and rewrote.

As always, thank you Tim, for the most constant and faithful support I could ever hope for.

INTRODUCTION

This book is for the busy manager who uses brainstorming as a tool to gather input and ideas from his or her staff. Here's what you can expect:

Each activity takes less than 15 minutes. Brainstorming is a quick process. Part of the success comes from the tight time limits you will impose on the session. You can get great results in minimal time. There's no need to linger on a topic until you've squeezed every last idea out of the group. Use these activities and the best ideas will flow quickly.

Each activity can be done with only a few basic materials. Most of these are things that your organization already has on hand: flip charts, markers, index cards, pens, and paper. You will need a stopwatch, but you can probably use the one on your cell phone. Other than that, the rest of the activities' supply lists include things that are not difficult to obtain: large sticky pads, balloons, magazines, and so on.

Each activity has a specific, focused purpose. Some are better for large groups, some for small groups. Some draw out quieter participants. Some are competitive. Some are faster paced than others. You can pick and choose which activities you use based on the needs of your group.

Each activity can be run by you, the busy manager. They are simple to understand and easy to plan and prepare for. Some of them can even be done successfully just moments after you read them for the first time. You take this book to your meeting and use a brainstorming activity right then and there!

The outline of each activity is easy to follow. Each one is presented in the same easy-to-read bulleted format:

This is . . . explains very briefly what the activity is.

What it does . . . tells the benefits of the activity and what it will help you accomplish, but it also includes a word of caution about a potential downside of using the activity.

What you need . . . tells you everything you'll need for the activity. Usually, it's nothing more than a marker and some flip chart paper, or a stack of index cards!

Here's how . . . tells you, step-by-step, how to conduct the activity.

For example . . . gives examples of things to use and/or shows how the activity may play out, so you get a good sense of what to expect. Often, there is an illustration at the end of the activity to show you how it will look on the chart or in the room when you are finished.

Tips for success . . . includes pointers and cautions that will help you run the activity more effectively.

Try these variations . . . offers variations on the activity that may slow it down, speed it up, expand or contract the scope, add a level of competition, or otherwise alter it for a slightly different brainstorming experience.

Relax, you won't find any of these kinds of activities here:

No "touchy-feely" activities in which participants have to touch each other a lot, or share personal thoughts or feelings with one another.

No outdoor activities that require large areas, nice weather, and physically fit participants.

No special handouts to prepare, copy, or distribute.

No lengthy activities during which more time is spent explaining the rules or warming the group up. Each activity takes about 15 minutes or less!

Before we get to the activities, though, there are three chapters that will help you be successful in *any* brainstorming session.

The first chapter explains what brainstorming is. It gives a brief history of brainstorming and some of the most common reasons for using it. You'll learn the four basic rules for brainstorming and why each is so important: focus on quantity not quality; don't allow criticism; encourage wild, outlandish ideas; combine ideas for more ideas. Then we'll look at the 10 steps of conducting a brainstorming session—from the planning and preparation, through implementation, and on to action planning for the future. Lastly, we'll take a look at the most common problems that arise in brainstorming sessions. We will consider ways to prevent them from happening in the first place, but we will also discuss what to do if they happen in spite of your best efforts.

In Chapter 2, we learn how to ask a great starting question to kick off the group's brainstorming. This first question focuses the group's energy and leads them to their own great responses. So it's got to be good, and it will be if you use their language, make it personal for them, keep it within scope, and use imagery to evoke responses. Once they start contributing, there are three ways to keep the energy high and the ideas flowing: using prompts, playback, and helping if necessary. We explore each of these techniques in detail in Chapter 2.

Chapter 3 looks at how to record your participants' responses. There is great power in the pen—you can make or break your brainstorming session just by what you record, or how you record your participants' input. You'll learn how to follow the four rules of recording: keep it moving, keep it theirs, keep it legible, and keep it organized.

Each of the first three chapters ends with a brief summary, and then a checklist that you can use to gauge how well you are applying the principles contained therein.

With these basics, you'll be ready for the brainstorming activities. There are four kinds of activities in this book, presented in four different chapters.

Chapter 4 includes a dozen activities for brainstorming, including the original, traditional method developed by Alex Osborn, the father of brainstorming. Each of the other activities has a slightly different focus or objective, so use them as your needs vary. Sometimes, the creativity of a group needs to be primed. For that, you can use the activities in Chapter 5 in tandem with the activities here.

Chapter 5 has almost 20 activities for encouraging more creativity from your participants during brainstorming. You may combine one of these exercises with an activity from Chapter 4. The activity from Chapter 4 gives the framework—the structure—to the brainstorming session, while the exercise from Chapter 5 will promote creativity from the participants as they use that structure.

Chapter 6 has several methods for categorizing or grouping the list of input your group will generate using the activities in Chapters 4 and 5. Often the list is so long that the participants need to group the input before they can even try to use the data meaningfully. These activities will help you do just that. This is an interim step for the group—after the list is generated, and before the data is analyzed and put to use.

Finally, Chapter 7 presents several processes for prioritizing the list generated earlier. This may mean ranking the ideas, or deciding on the best one, or simply sorting them into a few layers of importance. Because of the nature of group decision making, plan on these activities taking longer. The more important the issue, and the more participants involved, the longer it will take for everyone to feel heard, validated, and committed to a final resolution.

Brainstorming can be fun *and* productive! Enjoy using these activities to bring out the best from your team.

CHAPTER 1

BRAINSTORMING 101

Creative power can be stepped up by effort, and there are ways in which we can guide our creative thinking.

—ALEX OSBORN, THE FATHER OF BRAINSTORMING

What Is Brainstorming?

Brainstorming is a tool used to generate creative solutions to a problem. It was developed in the mid-1900s by a Madison Avenue advertising executive, Alex Osborn. He described it as "a conference technique by which a group attempts to find a solution for a specific problem by amassing all the ideas spontaneously by its members."

Brainstorming combines lateral thinking with a relaxed, informal approach. It uses a set of rules or techniques that encourage team members to come up with ideas, which are at times absurd, bizarre, or ridiculous! Some of the craziest ideas, however, can be crafted into workable, original solutions to the problem. Or, they may spark still more ideas from the group that are themselves more workable.

Why Use Brainstorming?

Brainstorming encourages members of a team to break out of their stale, overused, and established patterns of thinking. Fresh, unique, and different solutions are sought out for problems old and new. Brainstorming jolts team members out of the "tried and true," which is no longer working, and into uncharted, creative territory.

Brainstorming brings out and leverages the diverse experience and creativity of all team members. If two heads are better than one, imagine how much better a whole team of heads will be!

Brainstorming involves everyone. Team members feel included, which boosts morale. And since they were part of the solution, they are much more inclined to buy into that solution.

Brainstorming builds camaraderie and teamwork. Differences are not only respected, but welcomed and encouraged. Team members bond with one another because there's a feeling of respect and inclusiveness that pulls them together for a common purpose.

Brainstorming avoids problems associated with traditional group problem solving. Big egos are left at the door. Authority in the room is neutralized. Less assertive team members are included, even encouraged to participate. Pressure to come up with a total, complete, and flawless solution is relieved. Groupthink—where team members, in an attempt to avoid conflict, reach consensus without really evaluating options—is minimized; team members are freed up to think "outside the box."

Best of all, brainstorming is fun! It provides a positive, upbeat, and affirming experience for the team. And this carries over into regular day-to-day work.

What Are the Basic Rules of Brainstorming?

There are four basic rules for brainstorming. These are meant to reduce social inhibitions among team members, stimulate idea generation, and improve the overall creativity of the team's work.

Rule #1: Focus on quantity, not quality (quantity will lead to quality later).

> We need to think up plenty of tentative ideas, because, in ideation, quantity helps breed quality   —ALEX OSBORN

During a brainstorming session, the focus is entirely on quantity. There will be time later to qualify, or judge, the ideas, but for now, it's all about quantity. Everything should be aimed at generating more and more ideas, regardless of their quality. The underlying belief is that it's easier to pick good ideas (later) from a larger list than from a shorter one. It's easier to evaluate or modify an idea (later) than it is to create a new one.

A fast-paced session focused on quantity reduces the likelihood of team members trying to evaluate ideas prematurely (see Rule #2 below).

It also promotes uninhibited thinking, which leads to wild, outlandish ideas (see Rule #3 below)—and in the context of brainstorming, outlandish is good.

And, participants will find it fairly easy then to create good ideas by combining lots of little ideas (see Rule #4 below).

Keep the ideas short. Don't discuss the details of any idea. Just capture its essence and move on to the next idea quickly. With the focus off the idea itself, team members will feel less pressure to come up with "good ideas," "complete solutions," or those that are "well thought out."

Think fast, reflect later.

Rule #2: Withhold evaluation (at least for now).

We should hold back criticism until the creative current has had every chance to flow. —ALEX OSBORN

For most people, this is the most difficult rule. Hold off passing judgment on the ideas until after the brainstorming session is complete. This means no comments of how an idea is not feasible or what its downside is. While brainstorming, consider all ideas equally valid, and keep moving. This practice helps reduce inhibition in the team members, which then prompts greater quantity (see Rule #1).

Critiquing ideas takes brain power that could and should be devoted to idea generation.

Even positive reinforcement is taboo during brainstorming. If someone's idea gets lauded, what kind of pressure might that person feel to come up with another "good" idea? And how will the next person feel if their idea is not praised?

Every idea may be a great solution. It may also spark another, different idea that may be a great solution (see Rule #4). Yes, even the silliest ideas can spark better ones. Judgment is strictly forbidden, so the good and the seemingly not-so-good ideas emerge.

Once more: no evaluation! Reinforce this rule by writing everything that is said, no matter how ridiculous. A team member may say, "No, I was just kidding!" Write it anyway. The message is that there really is no such thing as a bad idea right now. Anything and everything is gladly accepted.

Rule #3: Encourage wild, outlandish ideas (nothing is too extreme . . . yet).

It is easier to tone down a wild idea than to think up a new one.
—Alex Osborn

Sometimes, the wilder and more outlandish the idea, the better. Sure, they may not make the cut when you do get to evaluating them, but often it's the bizarre and unworkable ideas that spark further ideas that turn out to be very doable indeed. It's easier to tame a wild idea into a valid solution than to try to boost a common idea into an original solution.

During brainstorming, no idea is too ridiculous or extreme. Raising the limits of acceptable ideas encourages team members to lower their inhibitions and generate more (see Rule #1) and better ideas. This is the rule that validates everyone's unique viewpoint and perspective.

Encourage out-of-the-box thinking. *Way* out of the box. Push for the exaggerated and the extreme. But in so doing, don't overlook the obvious. The plan is to keep everything a possibility for now.

Rule #4: Combine or build on ideas from others (because synergy means 1 + 1 = 3).

Most people have never learned . . . that they do possess the gift of creative imagination.
—Alex Osborn

Here's where the synergy of the group comes into play. Team members use each other's ideas as inspiration for more ideas. Build on them. Expand them. Combine them. Adapt them. Twist them. Add something to them. Improve them (without making mention of why the improvement, lest you violate Rule #2).

From this rule, wild ideas morph into viable, valuable solutions. How? The group assumes that every idea put forward has some merit, some truth, or some element that is useful. They seek out those nuggets of value and use them to come up with more ideas—ideas that others may yet be able to build upon even further!

This may feel like a free-for-all, and to a degree, that's a good thing. An open exchange of ideas is best. Do maintain some sense of order, though. Don't let people talk over each other, dominate the conversation, or otherwise give participants reason to pull back.

Everyone should participate in the brainstorming. For some, it's easier to adapt someone else's idea than to generate a completely original one. Remind them that it's just as valuable to the team to be able to adapt and improve other people's ideas as it is to generate the initial idea that sets off those new trains of thought in the first place.

The reason for these four rules is simple: free everyone to be as creative—in their own way—as possible!

How Is a Brainstorming Session Conducted?

Brainstorming sessions are not complex, nor are they particularly difficult. Often they are a small part of a regular staff or planning meeting. Sometimes brainstorming may be the sole purpose. Regardless, planning is essential for everyone to enjoy a successful experience. Follow these simple steps to ensure a productive brainstorming session.

Step #1: Be clear on the purpose of the session.

If you can't articulate the purpose of the session, don't have it until you can! This purpose should drive everything about the session— from the invitee list to the activities you chose to the questions you ask. Keep the purpose simple and easy to understand so that everyone can quickly engage. Remember KISSS—keep it short, simple, straightforward! For example: find a way to improve our hiring process; identify the roadblocks to better customer service; develop a marketing strategy for a new product.

This step sets everyone up for success, so be very clear before proceeding any further!

Step #2: Select your participants carefully.

Invite people who care about the purpose to participate. Don't fill the room with only similar-thinking people, though. The more diverse the group, the more creative the thinking. Consider inviting "outsiders" you wouldn't typically think to include—people with such different perspectives that their wild ideas may be just the ones that jar the rest of the group to a breakout solution.

The ideal size of a brainstorming session isn't set in stone.

Certainly, you don't want so many participants that they have to fight to be heard, so it's best to stay under 15 or 20. If you have more than that, use one of the activities that will split the group into smaller teams to brainstorm, and then come back together to share your ideas with the larger group.

"Facilitator" should be your only role during brainstorming so you can focus your energy on the job of facilitating. If you must also contribute as a participant, be aware of the extra power you have as the facilitator who controls the flow of the conversation and the documentation. Take steps to not abuse that power: call out when you shift from one role to the other, so participants don't get confused; offer your ideas later, rather than earlier; and so on.

Step #3: Create your Focus Question and select the activities to use.

Use Chapter 2 to create your Focus Question—the question that launches the brainstorming session. This question sets the stage for the entire brainstorming activity, so put some time and effort into creating the best one for your group's purpose.

People react differently to brainstorming sessions. You may want to present them with the Focus Question ahead of time so those who need it will have time to collect their thoughts.

Then use later chapters in this book to determine which brainstorming activity(ies) you will use with your Focus Question.

Step #4: Gather the materials and prepare the room.

You want the environment to be conducive to creativity. Make it comfortable and relaxed. Lower the lighting so it's not so harsh; draw shades if the view is distracting. Perhaps provide some toys or interesting play objects to stimulate thinking. Be sure to have plenty of supplies for recording the session: markers, paper, tape, laptop battery power, sticky notes, etc.

Step #5: Kick off the session with an icebreaker.

Warm up the group with a quick, fun icebreaker. (You will find dozens of quick options in my book *Quick Meeting Openers for Busy Managers*.) This will get the creative juices flowing and warm the participants to each other. Set the mood for the upcoming brainstorming to be fun, lively, and very interactive.

Step #6: Set the context and the boundaries for a successful brainstorming session.

First, review the purpose of the session with the team (which you can articulate brilliantly, because you did your homework back in Step #1). Make sure that everyone understands and buys into the challenge ahead of them.

Next, go over the four rules of brainstorming (see Figure 1–1). Do not assume that everyone knows them. And even if they say they do, the rules bear repeating anyway. Review them together. For each rule, emphasize its purpose to reinforce its necessity. Agree upfront how you or the group should handle violations. For example, what will you (or they) do if someone starts criticizing ideas? Get verbal or visual agreement from everyone in the room to abide by the four brainstorming rules before going forward.

Many facilitators set a time limit for the brainstorming session. This time pressure may add to the frantic pace in a good way. It may also be too much stress for the participants. Use your knowledge of the group to determine if a time limit would work or not.

Step #7: Set up the activity and ask the Focus Question.

If you are using an activity from this book, follow those instructions to get going. Then use your Focus Question to get the participants contributing. It should be succinct, specific, and targeted. See Chapter 2 for details of how to frame your question so it promotes the greatest response from your participants.

Step #8: Keep the session moving.

This step involves three actions that will ensure the session remains lively and engaging. First, record *every* idea offered. More on this in Chapter 3.

Second, keep the energy high and the ideas flowing. More on this in Chapter 2.

And finally, reinforce adherence to the rules of brainstorming outlined above. Nothing shuts down a session quicker than unchecked violations of these basic rules.

FIGURE 1-1

Brainstorming can be taxing work, though. If the task is large, break up the session into shorter periods of time so you don't burn the group out. Never go more than 15–20 minutes without changing course a bit or taking a break. Breaks can be a short 60-second stretch break, or a moment of silence to rejuvenate. Take your clues on when to break from the energy of the group.

Step #9: Process the list(s) as appropriate.

There's no point brainstorming a list of ideas if nothing is to be done with the list. Typically the next step is to categorize the list, prioritize it, or otherwise analyze it. Use the activities in Chapters 6 and 7 to accomplish this now, or plan for such actions to be done at a later date.

Step #10: Agree on next steps.

Wrap up the session by agreeing what the next steps will be. This includes how the ideas will be documented and when and with whom they will be shared. And finally, thank the group for their participation.

What Could Go Wrong?

Brainstorming sessions tend to be pretty straightforward, productive, and fun. But they aren't without minor hazards. Here are five of the most common pitfalls with some suggestions of how to handle them.

Pitfall #1: People are reluctant to fully participate.

This occurs if the environment feels threatening to them.

- ► Reinforce the basic rules of brainstorming, especially the prohibition on evaluation and criticism.
- ► Stop any criticism in the group—not just verbal comments (including groans and sighs), but facial expressions (rolling of eyes) and body language, too.
- ► Use an activity that splits the group into smaller teams so participants feel safer.
- ► Change the activity, perhaps using one where participants write (anonymously) their ideas first.

- ▶ Consider removing offending participants, or speaking to them during a break.
- ▶ Ask the group how the session could be improved.
- ▶ Check your own reactions: are you subtly critiquing (including positive rewards) their ideas, and thus contributing to the problem?

Pitfall #2: The same ideas are repeated over and over.

This may happen when a spectacular idea was given and the participants can't seem to get off it. Or, people are just worn out and have nothing left to give.

- ▶ Make sure the idea has been recorded adequately; remind them that it has already been captured.
- ▶ Change the activity, perhaps using a different one from Chapter 5 to redirect their creative juices.
- ▶ Take a stretch break or even a full time-out break (if the group seems tired).
- ▶ Have them change seats or otherwise shake up the environment to rejuvenate them.

Pitfall #3: They seem to struggle too much for new ideas; too much silence.

Periods of silence (while they think) are expected, but sometimes your participants will just get stuck.

- ▶ Change the activity to get their creativity going again.
- ▶ Do an icebreaker to help lower inhibitions and/or jump-start the group.
- ▶ Take a stretch break or even a full time-out break (if the group seems tired).
- ▶ Tell the group that silent periods are a normal part of brainstorming.
- ▶ Remain positive yourself, comfortable with the momentary silence, smile reassuringly.
- ▶ Play light music in the background throughout the session to fill any awkward moments of silence.
- ▶ Don't feel compelled to break the silence (and rescue the group)— let them wrestle and come out of it together, stronger!

Pitfall #4: Someone dominates the session.

Distinguish between those who are truly dominating and those who are merely loud and excited but still very helpful and respectful.

- ▶ Encourage others to participate verbally as well as nonverbally (make eye contact, nod your head, use hand gestures, etc.).
- ▶ Change the activity; perhaps use a different one that regulates how people participate, or that splits them into smaller teams.
- ▶ Ask them to hold off briefly while others (more shy, less assertive, quieter types, etc.) contribute.
- ▶ Take a break and speak to the offending participant(s) privately about how their high enthusiasm may be inhibiting others.

Pitfall #5: The worst: no solution is found.

The whole purpose of a brainstorming session is to resolve something. Imagine the disappointment if that goal is not accomplished!

- ▶ Check that everyone (especially you!) was clear on the purpose or goal.
- ▶ Evaluate if the brainstorming session was mismanaged somehow. Did you follow the steps above? Was the environment encouraging? Did you have the right invitees? And so on.
- ▶ Ask the group what went wrong.
- ▶ Determine how you can salvage any of the work done toward a true resolution of the issue.
- ▶ Check if brainstorming was the right process to address this particular issue in the first place.

Summary

Brainstorming uses a set of rules to help a team create solutions to problems that otherwise go unresolved. They key is to begin with many, many ideas (some of which may be outlandish) and build an even longer list before critiquing anything.

There are four basic rules of brainstorming:

1. Focus on quantity, not quality—for now.
2. Hold off on critiquing or judging ideas until later. This includes refraining from positive comments as well.
3. Nothing is too extreme yet, so encourage wild, outlandish ideas.

4. Leverage the synergy of the group to create new ideas from the ideas being given.

There's a right way and a not-so-right way to conduct a brainstorming session. Follow these 10 simple steps:

1. Get clear on the session's purpose; don't proceed until you do.
2. Invite the appropriate participants, including some with different perspectives.
3. Create the Focus Question and identify the activities to use.
4. Gather the materials needed.
5. Begin the session with an appropriate icebreaker.
6. Set the context and the boundaries for a successful session by reviewing the rules of brainstorming.
7. Set up the activity and ask your Focus Question.
8. Keep the session moving with prompts and encouragement.
9. Process the lists of ideas generated right then, or at a later date.
10. Agree on next steps and commit to them.

As you already know full well, things rarely go as smoothly as you wish. Anticipate the following five common problems and be prepared to address them:

1. People are reluctant to participate.
2. The same ideas are repeated over and over.
3. Too much silence.
4. Someone dominates the session.
5. No resolution is found.

This summary has just given you the really, really short version of Brainstorming 101. You will probably want to read this chapter before every brainstorming session you conduct until it becomes second nature.

CHAPTER 2

IT ALL STARTS WITH A QUESTION

A paradigm shift occurs when a question is asked inside the current paradigm that can only be answered from outside it.

—MARILEE GOLDBERG, *THE ART OF THE QUESTION*

Every brainstorming session begins with a question. The better the question, the better the responses. The better the responses, the better the outcome of the session. It's just that simple!

A good starting question sets up the group to participate freely. It will focus the group's energy on the brainstorming for the greatest productivity. It will even lead them to their answers. For example, if you are gathering information, it will help them call to mind the data needed. If you are looking for ideas, it will get their creative juices flowing in the right direction.

So any old question will not do. It needs to be a Focus Question. And not just any old Focus Question—it needs to be a *good* Focus Question! And that's exactly what you learn to develop in this chapter.

Use Focus Questions to Kick Off a Successful Brainstorming Session

Typically, when you run a brainstorming session, you know what information you are after. With that in mind, you can easily create a starting question aimed at your specific need. However, that's not really enough: what you need is a question that will help your *participants!*

Say your goal is to improve your organization's budget approval process. You determine that the first step is to fully understand how the process works now: what goes into getting a department's budget approved. You assemble a team of department heads who have experienced the current budgeting process. Your starting question may be simple, and very straightforward:

What inputs are required to get a budget approved?

This starting question serves your needs nicely, but not your participants'. Yes, it is direct and to the point, but it will fall flat when you ask your team of department heads. It's conceptual and theoretical. They will have to work to get to the answers you seek—answers based in reality. You may even wind up helping them by rephrasing the question, or (worse) throwing out a few possible responses to "prime the pump." Now your open-ended question has become a multiple-choice question—and that's not brainstorming.

A better approach is to do more work beforehand to create a superior starting question, called a Focus Question. Look at the two examples below. Which one would elicit more (and better) responses from your team of department heads?

1. *What inputs are required to get a budget approved?*
2. *Think back to last year's budgeting process. Remember everything you submitted for your capital budget request. You probably had to go to multiple sources for the stuff you needed. Perhaps your request was even rejected pending more information or documentation. So, let's start a list. What are the things you had to provide to get your capital budget approved?*

Obviously the second one will pull out more and better responses. Unlike a typical starting question, it's got four essential elements that make it a great Focus Question. We'll explore each of these elements below, and see how each one improves the original starting question.

Essential element #1: Use the participants' language.

Participants can (and will) engage quicker when they don't have to translate your terms into theirs. Recall the example above:

What inputs are required to get a budget approved?

The term "inputs required" may be obvious to you, but not to your participants. To them it may mean the budget form online only. If so, they won't bring up all the supporting documentation. And what about signatures, do you want them to say that, too?

So translate your terms into their language. Make it easy to understand exactly what you are after. In our example, the starting question could be rephrased this way:

What information needs to be entered into the system to get a budget approval?

Notice how the question is more easily understood because it's colloquial for the participants. They don't have to *try* to understand it; it already makes sense to them. They can begin contributing immediately.

Essential element #2: Make it personal.

Participants can (and will) engage more enthusiastically when the question is about them—not about you, not about the organization. From the example above, we have:

What information needs to be entered into the system to get a budget approval?

Upon hearing this question, participants may think they are supposed to give you answers that are about what should happen (not how it is), or horror stories they have heard of how it happened to someone (not them, today). Change the question from third person to second person to make it about them:

What information do you need to enter into the system to get your budget approved?

The focus is now off the generalizations of shoulds and once-upon-a-times, and onto the participants' actual experiences, where it belongs. They don't have to conceptualize at all; they are invited to share their own experiences, which is what you wanted all along.

Essential element #3: Stay within scope.

Participants can (and will) engage more effectively—be more on target with their responses—when the question keeps them within the true scope of the problem or opportunity they face. Here's our example again so far:

What information do you need to enter into the system to get your budget approved?

Before launching a discussion with this question, think about the scope of the question. What assumptions have been made here? What decisions or limits (or freedoms) are implied here? In this example, the term "information" may be too limiting. It implies data to some. And the phrase "enter into the system" excludes special documentation that is outside the online budget form. If you want more information, broaden your question language to get a broader set of responses from your participants.

What do you need to provide *to get your budget approved?*

But as you consider this question, you also realize that most of the budgeting process is very straightforward. It's quite routine: operating expenses, labor, admin and office supplies, travel, etc. The real concern here is the capital budgeting process. So let's narrow the question so you can limit participant responses to only what's truly relevant for your situation.

What do you need to provide to get your capital budget *approved?*

Now the question solicits responses that are within the true scope of your goal. First, your participants can volunteer more than just the data they plug into the spreadsheets because the question has been expanded to invite that. Second, they aren't going to waste time talking about routine (and irrelevant for this case) information that is not related to capital budgets because the question has also been tightened up to exclude that.

Essential element #4: Evoke responses.

Participants will engage passionately when the question encourages them to reflect on, and then share, their own reality. Our example question now reads:

What do you need to provide to get your capital budget approved?

Lead them to their answers by painting a picture for them to reflect upon. Remind them of the last time they went through this process, and then ask them to share their results relevant to your discussion.

Think back to last year's budgeting process. Remember everything you submitted for your capital budget request. You probably had to go to multiple sources for the stuff you needed. Perhaps your request was even rejected pending more information or documentation. So, let's start a list. What are the things you had to provide to get your capital budget approved?

Notice how the first sentence starts with an image-building phrase that begins with "Think back . . .". Other image-building words include: remember, consider, go back, recall, etc. If your group is tasked with generating creative ideas rather than a list of concrete things, as in this example, image-building phrases might include words like imagine, what about, if, pretend for a moment, think about, etc.

Once you've created an image for them to reflect on, extend that image so they can actually see their responses, as we do in the second and third sentences. Lead them there, but don't give them the answers. Just take them far enough so they see their answers.

Then, finally, ask your question (final sentence) and wait for all the responses.

A word of caution here: Make sure that the image you give your participants is the one that will lead them to relevant responses. Using the same scenario as above, consider this starting question:

Think back to last year's budgeting process. Remember all the things you had going on at the same time. Recall how you felt when the announcement came out that it was time to do budgets, and how little time you felt like you had to do this. So let's start a list. What are the things you had to provide to get your capital budget approved?

With *this* introduction, we've created an image centered around the timing of the budgeting cycle and how this added to your participants' stress level last year. It has nothing to do with the inputs to the capital budgeting process. So when the question does come, it's a bit jarring, as if it's from out of the blue. The imagery is a distraction rather than a help. Be sure your imagery leads *to* the question, not *away* from it.

Using Focus Questions for Idea Generation

Focus Questions are good for brainstorming ideas as well as for creating lists, as we saw above. Let's explore an example of this. Assume we've already used the Focus Question above to uncover how the current capital budgeting process works. We then would use a different Focus Question to identify as many of the trouble spots as possible. Finally, it's time to brainstorm some creative possibilities to improve, or fix, the process. The initial starting question may be:

What system enhancements are necessary for the capital budget approval process?

First, let's make sure we're using the participants' language. Consider the word "enhancements." To the Information Technology department it's obvious this means *any* kind of change to the system.

But your department heads may interpret this to mean only *additions* to the system, making it bigger, broader, and possibly even *more* cumbersome. They may not consider options that would *omit* or *modify*. So we change the wording to make better sense to them:

How could the system be improved *for the capital budget approval process?*

Now let's make it personal for the department heads in the room:

How could we improve the system for your *capital budget approvals?*

Next, we check the scope of the question. This question limits the discussion to ideas only about the system. What about solutions that don't involve the system at all? We'll expand the question to encourage participants to think beyond the system.

How can we improve the way *that your capital budgets get approved?*

Finally, let's lead them to their answers with some imagery around the possibilities.

Think about what it would be like if the capital budget process was a delight, rather than a burden. You complete your request for a capital budget and relish how painless, simple, and quick it all was. Certainly an improvement over prior years! Technology made a difference, but it wasn't the only thing that changed for the better. Let your mind wander, and see possibilities that may not even seem feasible. Let's list all these great ideas you're having. How could we improve the way that your capital budgets get approved?

A Final Note About Focus Questions

Brainstorming sessions often require more than one Focus Question. Each agenda item may need to begin with a Focus Question. If you were dealing with the situation in the examples above, you might use three Focus Questions for your session. The first example above showed how to help the team identify the current inputs to the capital budget process. Next, you would have used a Focus Question (no example was given) to call out the trouble spots and/or root causes in the current process. And then the last example above would help the team generate a list of potential solutions. Notice how you don't need to know the answers to the first Focus Question to be able to prepare effective Focus Questions for later points of the agenda.

Come to the session with well-prepared Focus Questions and you'll be rewarded with much higher engagement and much higher quality of results!

Keep the Ideas Flowing After the Focus Question

Once you put the Focus Question out there, your participants will start responding. So how do you keep their ideas coming? There are three general methods to do this, all of which are question-based. Statements shut a group down quickly. Questions keep them engaged and participating.

Prompts

Actively solicit more input with gentle (or not so gentle!) prompts. While prompts help your group get over a lull, don't feel like you have to wait for that lull to use them. They can be great lull-preventers. Brainstorming is most effective when the energy stays high and the pace is brisk, so use prompts liberally. Here are some simple prompts:

- What else?
- Anything else?
- Keep 'em coming!
- Thank you!
- And?
- More, please?
- Another one?
- Yes!
- Who else?
- Anyone else?

Resist the temptation to use prompts like "good one" or "I like that." They seem like positive reinforcement, but really they violate the rules of brainstorming. They are evaluative or judgmental and may shut down some participants. What if their comment isn't so "good"? Some participants may even begin to compete for your approval.

NOTE: There is a distinct difference between the first two prompts above. "What else?" is an open question. The number of possible responses is limitless. It assumes there *are* more responses in the group and participants are invited to share them. "Anything else?" is a closed question. The only valid responses are yes and no. Human nature is such that most will answer no, and be done. Use these two questions deliberately: the first when you want to encourage more discussion, the second when you want to close things down and move on to the next agenda item (and yes, that time will come).

The same correlation exists between the last two prompts above. "Who else?" invites more participants to share what they have. "Anyone else" feels like you're allowing a final contribution before moving on.

Playback

Play back what you hear. Your participants will engage (or stay engaged) when they believe they are being heard. Acknowledge their participation by playing back what they've said. Paraphrase the last thing you heard and check with whoever said it to confirm that you got it right.

It sounds like what you're saying is . . . Is that right?

Another form of playback is particularly effective when a group stalls. Sometimes just hearing a few (or all!) of their ideas again will jump-start their creativity and off they go. You can do this a couple of ways. One is to read a few random things listed and then ask for more.

So we've heard things like X, Y, and Z. What else is there?

Or, you may reread (or paraphrase) the entire list and then ask for more.

Let's see. We have A, B, C, D, E, F, G, and H. Great list so far, let's keep going!

CAUTION: These latter two playback techniques can feel redundant if overused. Use them sparingly, and only when the group has stalled. High energy in your voice will keep this kind of playback from boring the participants.

Help

Another tool to use when a group gets stuck is to help them see something that they are missing. This is a tricky space for you if you are not also filling the role of a participant. If you start throwing out ideas as facilitator, you risk being perceived as trying to usurp the group's power, or even as driving your own agenda. But if you stay quiet about an important idea, you prevent the group from being its most effective.

To help, start by asking a question that points the participants toward the idea they are missing. This is called a leading question, because you are leading them to a realm of answers.

Are there solutions in the area of . . . ?

Who else may be impacted by this and what might they say?

What alternatives may exist?

Is there a way to get X and Y and still accomplish what we want?

If, and only if, your leading question doesn't work, and the group is still missing something key, float an idea using these three guidelines. First, offer the idea in the form of a question. This gets the idea out for discussion. Then ask a direct question about the merits of the idea. This helps the group begin to take ownership of what started as your idea. Finally, ask them how you should write the new idea. By rewording the idea for recording, the group solidifies its ownership of that idea.

If at any point along the way the group resists, let it go! Don't let your temporary ego get in the way of their overall success. Don't argue or defend your idea, just let it go.

Let's revisit our example about improving the budget process, and see how asking a leading question or floating an idea may help. Perhaps you see that they are missing the critical connection between their capital budgets and the Facilities department. You begin with a leading question:

Have we considered everyone that has a say on your budgets?

Or even a little more leading:

How might the Facilities department be part of our solution?

If this doesn't get at how the current process ignores Facilities, right up until the moment they exercise their veto power at the end of the process, the three steps of floating an idea may look like this:

What if we brought Facilities into the budget preparation process before we get to the final approval? (You float the idea in the form of a question.)

You hope to get responses on the order of, "Yes! That's a great idea!" And you go on to ask:

How might that benefit you? (You ask a direct question inviting the group to consider owning the idea.)

The participants might respond with something like, "Well, we'd avoid that feeling of 'gotcha' at the end. We'd also be able to be more realistic in our requests before we even submit them, so we wouldn't get our hopes up unnecessarily."

OK, so how would you like me to write this? (You ask how to record the idea so they can claim it as theirs, not yours.)

The key to asking leading questions and floating ideas is leaving your ego out of it. Taking credit for helping the group keeps them from owning whatever ideas came up (whether they were your brilliant ideas to begin with, or theirs as a result of your brilliant questioning). Once the group senses your ego involvement, they will resist your future efforts.

Putting It All Together

Using our example above, here's how you might use a Focus Question to get started, followed by how you might keep the brainstorming session going (remember, you want to leave time between sentences—you want their minds to start to wander in the direction you are sending them):

FACILITATOR: *Think about what it would be like if the capital budget process was a delight, rather than a drag.* (Pause.) *You complete your request for a capital budget and relish how painless, simple, and quick it all was. Certainly an improvement over prior years!* (Pause.) *Technology made a difference, but it wasn't the only thing that changed for the better. Go ahead, let your mind wander, and see possibilities that may not even seem feasible right away.* (Pause.) *Let's list all these great ideas you're having. How could we improve the way that your capital budgets get approved?*

PARTICIPANT 1: *Use more technology.*

PARTICIPANT 2: *Eliminate having to get HR to sign off on capital expenditures.*

FACILITATOR: *Keep 'em coming . . .*

PARTICIPANT 3: *How about if we start the process earlier in the year?*

FACILITATOR: *Say more about that, please.*

PARTICIPANT 3: *Well, they kick off the budget season in early June and expect it to be done by mid-July. For most of us that it's impossible, because so many of our key people take vacation then.*

FACILITATOR: *OK, thank you, what else?*

PARTICIPANT 4: *I'd love to see the cutoffs for what is and what is not a capital expense changed. They're just too low right now.*

FACILITATOR: *So you'd like to see the minimum raised, is that right?*

PARTICIPANT 4: *Yes, exactly!*

FACILITATOR: *OK, so we've got technology, raising limits, starting the process sooner in the year. Let's get a few more.*

PARTICIPANT 2: *Hmm, well, if the forms were simpler to fill out, I could delegate this to some of the people directly responsible for the budgets.*

FACILITATOR: *You mean they can't participate now?*

PARTICIPANT 2: *Well, I guess they can, but . . . actually, yes, it's that they can't sign off on the requests, so maybe that's what we should change.*

FACILITATOR: *So what I'm hearing you say is that we should change the sign-off limits so the people involved with the spending can operate without coming to you?*

PARTICIPANT 2: *Yes, that's it!*

PARTICIPANT 5: *Why not just get rid of spending limits altogether?! No! Wait. Don't write that, I was just kidding!*

FACILITATOR: (Writes the idea anyway.) *I'm wondering, have we considered everyone that has a say on your budgets?*

PARTICIPANT 3: *Someone already mentioned getting HR out of the process.*

FACILITATOR: *Yes, we did. And what about Facilities?*

PARTICIPANT 3: *What do you mean? They have to be involved, they have final say on it!*

FACILITATOR: *Well, what if we brought Facilities into the budget preparation process, before we get to the final approval?*

PARTICIPANT 7: *Yes! That's a great idea!*

FACILITATOR: *How might that benefit us?*

PARTICIPANT 7: *Well, we'd avoid that feeling of "gotcha" at the end.*

PARTICIPANT 1: *Yes, and we'd be able to be more realistic in our requests before we even submit them.*

PARTICIPANT 2: *And that it would be nice to not get our staffs' hopes up unnecessarily. That's just so frustrating!*

FACILITATOR: *OK, so how would you like me to write this?*

PARTICIPANT 6: *Involve Facilities during budget input.*

FACILITATOR: *Got it. Who's got another idea?*

Summary

The best starting question for a brainstorming session is a Focus Question. Focus Questions have four components:

1. Use the participants' own language—they will engage quicker if they don't have to translate your terms into theirs.

2. Make it personal—they will engage more enthusiastically when the question is about them, not you or the organization.

3. Stay within scope—participants will engage more effectively, and will be more on target with their responses, when the question keeps them within the true scope of the problem or opportunity.

4. Evoke responses with imagery—they will engage passionately when the question encourages them to reflect on and share their own reality.

Focus Questions are effective for generating lists and for conjuring ideas. It's important to keep up the momentum. Keep the brainstorming session alive with three techniques:

1. Actively solicit more input with gentle (or not so gentle!) prompts. *What else? Keep 'em coming!*

2. Play back what you are hearing. *What you're saying is . . ., right? So far we have X, Y, and Z, so what else is there?*

3. Offer help when you see the group overlooking something that is critical. Use leading questions first: *Are there options in the area of . . . ? What about this idea . . . ?* Float an idea as a last resort. After floating an idea, ask the group to expand on it, and then ask them how they want the idea to be written (so they take ownership of it).

This chapter introduced you to the art—yes, art—of developing great Focus Questions, questions that will ensure that you have a productive brainstorming session. In the next chapter you will see how to make sure that none of the wonderful ideas slip out of your grasp. Read on!

CHAPTER 3

THE POWER OF THE PEN

It is not deeds or acts that last: it is the written record of those deeds or acts.

—ELBERT HUBBARD (WRITER, PUBLISHER, PHILOSOPHER)

Ask a good Focus Question and your participants will start responding. That means you need to start recording those responses—immediately! The number of tools for recording responses continues to grow. Besides traditional flip chart or butcher paper, there are white boards, sticky notes, copy boards, laptop projections, web-based bulletin boards for virtual sessions, and many more. To choose which tool to use, consider the following:

- **Visibility**: How well will the recorded notes be visible to all participants? Will lights need to be dimmed? Can the notes be seen from the farthest seat in the room? How large does the writing or the font need to be for easy reading?

- **Competency**: How comfortable am I using this tool? Do I know how to operate it if it's a high-tech option? How legible is my writing? Which font is easiest for my participants to read? How will I handle technical difficulties if they arise?

- **Transferability**: How will I transfer the recorded notes into something I can share with my participants after the session?

- **Flexibility**: How will I correct, amend, delete, and otherwise deal with the recorded notes when we start categorizing, prioritizing, or otherwise analyzing them?

- **Portability**: How portable are the recorded notes? How "permanent" is each "page" of notes? How easily will we be able to refer back to prior "pages" of notes?

The Four Rules of Recording Brainstorming Sessions

Your Focus Question is important to get things started. But how you record your participants' responses will also have a tremendous impact on the success of your brainstorming session! There are four basic rules that will help you keep your session lively, creative, and productive.

Rule #1: Keep it moving.

Brainstorming is all about a free-flow of information and ideas. This happens when your participants feel safe and valued as they participate. Remember, in true brainstorming there are no wrong answers. Now is not the time to discuss the merits of a contribution, or if it even belongs on the list. It really doesn't matter if their comment is incomplete, inaccurate, or even irrelevant. No matter what they say, record it. No matter what it is, record it. Always!

This simple acknowledgment of their contribution will encourage them to continue participating. You can fix anything that needs fixing later. For now, just record—everything!

As stated in Chapter 2, be careful not to evaluate any comments as they are being made. This can't be stressed enough. Even reinforcing comments like "good one," "I like that," "I was hoping someone would say that," "wow, how creative," are absolutely off limits. An idea that doesn't garner praise may be deemed as not-good enough, not-exciting enough, or not-creative enough by the participants. Intimidated by that, they may opt out of further participation.

One trick for keeping the pace brisk is to start recording while they are still talking. If you wait for them to finish before you start recording, there will be "dead time" while they wait for you to catch up. This will sap the energy from the team and keep them from one of the benefits of true brainstorming—the creativity that comes from the speed and energy of the process.

There are a few other tricks to keep the session moving. Ask your prompt questions while you are still recording the last comment made. *What else? Who's got another one?* These prompts will let your participants know that it's okay to continue talking (and thinking!) as you record. You send them the message that you don't want them to hold up on your account. Too many or too long silent pauses are usually fatal to a good brainstorming session.

You may also use playback. Paraphrase back to them what you heard and/or what you are recording, as you record it. Another way is to ask them to repeat what they said so you can be sure to capture it accurately. The goal is to keep the energy in the room up while you're documenting what is said.

Rule #2: Keep it theirs.

In his landmark book *The Secrets of Facilitation* (Jossey-Bass, 2004), Michael Wilkinson urges facilitators to "write what *they* said, not what *you* heard." It's tempting to interpret, clarify, wordsmith, improve, or even salvage participant comments in an attempt to help. Don't do it! Changing even one of their words makes the remark yours, not theirs. And when you start making things yours, they stop contributing.

Editing their comments also sends the message that they are not competent to speak for themselves. Not only will this shut down some participants, it will encourage others to look for you to fix more and more of their comments. Soon, they will be expecting you to clean up their thinking for them.

And if you start to edit, certainly your participants have license to do the same. You don't want them "fixing" each other's contributions. This would shut down most people rather quickly!

You needn't record every word they say, though; you're not a stenographer. Record as many of *their own words* as is necessary to capture the essence of their thought. Get down enough of their words to ensure that the recording is complete; that it can be remembered or understood on its own. If they are long-winded or rambling, just ask them to give you the bottom line, "headline it," or otherwise summarize their thought so you can record it for them. *How would you like me to record that?* works quite nicely! Or, *how would you say that in five to seven words?*

Sometimes you may find that their words won't be enough for clarification of the final documentation. This situation is rare, but when it arises, use your own words sparingly. Ideally, use a different color ink for your words, or put them in parentheses.

Abbreviations are fine, so long as they are spelled out the first time you use each one. Don't assume you'll remember a clever abbreviation that you made up on the spot. Record it somewhere!

Remember: it's critical that you use *their* words, not yours.

Rule #3: Keep it legible.

What good are group notes if you and your participants can't see or read them?

It may seem too basic to mention, but the words should be large enough to be seen by everyone. If you write, make the letters straight and neat and distinct. The key here is to take your time. Don't rush!

Leave plenty of space between entries. Not only does this make the record easier to read, it also gives you room to add, amend, or even correct things when it's time to analyze the list.

Use dark colors (black, brown, blue, dark green, dark purple) that can be seen by everyone. Avoid yellow, orange, and other light colors. Red is difficult to read from a distance, but can be used effectively to highlight or emphasize if used sparingly. It's pleasing to most when the dark colors are alternated. Don't rely too heavily on color-coded entries though. The distinction between those dark colors may be difficult from a distance—and nearly 10 percent of men are color-blind.

That said, you may want to record all of your brainstorming session in just one or two colors. Then you can use a second or third color to categorize, prioritize, or analyze the input afterwards. This will help you distinguish the original comments from the changes.

Stay close to the board, laptop, or whatever tool you are using. This will save a few seconds in travel time to and from that tool. This may not seem like much, but even a few seconds of silence can start to drain the energy from a room. Don't let your movement get in the way of their flow of ideas.

Rule #4: Keep it organized.

Label everything—all your charts or pages or files, whatever you are using—beforehand or as you go (never after the fact). Then post them (preferably as you go along) so everyone can see them and refer back to them if they like. Each page of flip chart paper should be labeled at the top. Each section of a white board used should be labeled at the top. Same goes for each slide, screen, or bulletin board online. Every collection of sticky notes should be grouped and labeled.

A great way to keep your group notes organized for later is to do both: label and number the pages. Labeling will help you all keep the things recorded in perspective and in context. Numbering will help you later pull the notes together in the organized order of how they were created.

When it comes time to document the session, labeled charts or pages are invaluable, especially if someone other than you is creating the final document. Even if you are doing this yourself, don't assume you'll remember things accurately. You won't.

Don't depend on your memory to remember—label and number everything to be sure (see Figure 3-1).

FIGURE 3-1

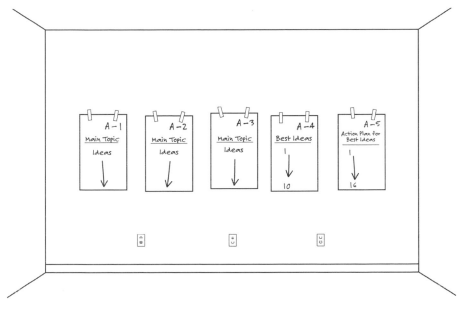

Summary

When choosing a tool for recording a brainstorming session, consider visibility, your own competency, transferability of the notes, flexibility of the tool, transportability of the notes, as well as what resources are available.

The four rules of recording brainstorming sessions are:

1. Keep it moving.

   a. No matter what they say, record it.
   b. No evaluation of their comments, not even positive comments.
   c. Start recording while they are still talking.

     d. Use prompts to solicit more responses while you're still recording the last one.

     e. Play back what you heard as you record to fill dead air.

     f. Ask participants to expand their comments while you record to clarify as well as to promote more creativity.

2. Keep it theirs.

     a. Record what they said, not what you heard.

     b. Don't "fix" anything they say; use their own words to document.

     c. Record as many of their words as necessary to capture the essence so it is understood on its own.

     d. It's okay to ask them how they want you to record their thought.

     e. Use your own words very sparingly—in different-colored ink or in parentheses.

     f. Spell abbreviations out at least once so you don't forget what they mean later.

3. Keep it legible.

     a. Record with large, neat, straight, distinct letters and words.

     b. Leave space between entries for readability and for changes to the document later.

     c. Use dark colors; avoid lighter colors and red (which are difficult to read).

     d. Use a different color later for changes to the original brainstorming comments.

     e. Keep yourself close to the recording tool to minimize downtime going to and from it.

4. Keep it organized.

     a. Label all charts, pages, screens, etc., to stay organized and maintain focus.

     b. Post everything as you go along so all work is visible to the group at all times.

     c. Number charts, pages, screens, etc. to make it easier to keep things in order for later transfers of the information.

Okay, enough with the rules. You must be eager to get to the meat of the matter—brainstorming techniques and activities, both traditional and novel. *Vamonos! Avanti!* Full steam ahead!

CHAPTER **4**

BRAINSTORMING TECHNIQUES

Use these activities to structure a brainstorming session. Time limits are just suggestions. Adjust them to fit your topic, your group, and your situation. Err on the side of brevity and adjust as necessary. It's better to extend the time because of too much engagement than to let the group run out of energy.

Chapter 5 has activities designed to improve the group's creativity in brainstorming. Combine them with these brainstorming techniques for a more creative session.

Chapter 6 has activities for sorting and grouping the responses from the brainstorming session. Use them after these techniques to organize the responses for further consideration or analysis.

Chapter 7 has activities for prioritizing the responses from the brainstorming session. Use them after these techniques to rank, separate out, or choose the best response(s).

TRADITIONAL BRAINSTORMING

This is . . .
- *The* traditional brainstorming technique upon which all other brainstorming techniques are based.

What it does . . .
- Encourages lots of responses in a nonthreatening environment.
- Provides participants with an activity that is familiar and comfortable.

One drawback is . . .
- Because of its familiarity, this activity may be misused by participants who forget or violate the rules.

What you need . . .
- One board (flip chart, white board, etc.) and a marker.
- A stopwatch or timer.

Here's how . . .
1. Review the purpose of the session with the group.
2. Review and get agreement on the four rules of brainstorming (see Chapter 1).
3. Ask the Focus Question and start the clock.
4. Record their responses on the board.
5. Sort or prioritize using the methods in Chapter 6 or 7.

Tips for success . . .
- This activity works best with groups up to about 12–15 participants. Larger groups will overwhelm you unless you have an assistant recording the responses with you.

- Set a time limit that seems too short at first. It's better to have responses left over (and then have to extend the time) than the other way around. Generally, don't go longer than 15–20 minutes, though.
- Emphasize the rules of brainstorming and enforce them! While most people are familiar with this traditional approach, many are not used to being held to the "no critiquing" rule. This is especially true for those who want to make positive comments, as well as those who want to eliminate the truly outlandish responses (which may very well prompt great, realistic responses later!).

Try these variations . . .
- Combine this technique with any of the creativity exercises in Chapter 5.

STICKIES

This is . . .
➤ A brainstorming technique where participants record their own responses on large stickies first, before posting them on a larger board for everyone to see.

What it does . . .
➤ Gives everyone a chance to participate at their own pace, and in a noncompetitive environment.
➤ Helps neutralize some of the more dominant members of the group.
➤ Allows the responses to be very easily moved around when sorted or prioritized later.

One drawback is . . .
➤ This activity slows down the brainstorming as it takes more time to write than to speak.

What you need . . .
➤ Pads of large (3" x 5" or larger) stickies.
➤ A marker for each participant.
➤ A stopwatch or timer.

Here's how . . .
1. Review the purpose of the session with the group.
2. Review and get agreement on the four rules of brainstorming (see Chapter 1).
3. Distribute a marker and a stack of stickies to each participant.
4. Explain that they will have 2 minutes to individually write on their stickies as many responses to the Focus Question as they can.
5. Explain that each response goes on its own separate sticky.
6. Ask the Focus Question and start the clock.

7. After time is up, have the participants read their stickies aloud and post them on the wall.
8. As they hear others' stickies, they may get more ideas—write them down!
9. Sort or prioritize using the methods in Chapter 6 or 7.

Tips for success . . .

► This activity is great for groups that are somewhat familiar with brainstorming, but wary of the competitive or more unconventional techniques found later in this book.

► This activity works well for most groups, although larger groups may get bored or overwhelmed with all the reading of stickies.

► Have participants take turns reading their stickies one at a time, so no one dominates.

► Encourage participants to discard duplicate stickies, but only if they are truly identical to someone else's.

► Since the group will use the stickies to later sort or prioritize, encourage legible writing.

► Using index cards and tape instead of sticky notes can work just fine.

► Encourage participants to fit their response on the sticky using the marker, not a pen. This will force them to keep their responses short and to the point.

Try these variations . . .

► Split the group into teams. Give a marker and stack of stickies to each team. Have the team choose a scribe who will capture all their responses (including his or her own). Then proceed as outlined above.

► Have participants post their stickies randomly around the room. Read (or have the participants take turns reading) each of the stickies. Participants should continue to write and post stickies when they are inspired by the other stickies. Note: this helps separate participants from their responses, but does not guarantee anonymity.

► Give each participant, or each small team, a certain number of stickies and require them to think of that many responses.

BUBBLES

This is . . .
- A brainstorming technique where participants put their initial responses into eight bubbles, and then build on those ideas further.

What it does . . .
- Offers the group a structured, organized, and visual approach.
- Helps participants see and/or build upon the relationships and connections among their responses.
- Keeps the group motivated to come up with more responses to fill the bubbles.

One drawback is . . .
- It may feel like the brainstorming is contrived or forced beyond reason, just for the sake of filling in bubbles.

What you need . . .
- One large board (flip chart, white board, etc.) and a marker.

Here's how . . .
1. Review the purpose of the session with the group.
2. Review and get agreement on the four rules of brainstorming (see Chapter 1).
3. Draw three rows of three empty circles (bubbles); write the topic in the center bubble.
4. Ask the Focus Question.
5. Record the first eight responses in the surrounding bubbles.
6. Draw more sets of nine bubbles. Each of the original eight responses goes in the center of one of those new sets of bubbles.

7. The group then brainstorms more responses based on those new center bubbles (always relating back to the original topic). See Figure 4–1 for an example of what this might look like.
8. Sort or prioritize using the methods in Chapter 6 or 7.

Tips for success . . .
- Tape lots of sets of bubbles to a wall beforehand so they are ready for use as you need them (instead of having to slow down the brainstorming to draw as you go).
- Don't limit yourself to one iteration of bubbles. For example, one idea may prompt eight responses, and only two of those responses may prompt eight more, and one of those may prompt even more.
- Don't feel compelled to explore all eight bubbles equally. Follow the energy of the group.
- Allow the group to move to new sets of bubbles before they've completed the original eight. Only force them to finish all eight bubbles before moving on if you want to encourage a rigid discipline to their brainstorming.
- Once they complete the original set of bubbles, remind the group of the topic often, so they don't get distracted or go off task with succeeding iterations.
- Allow extra time for this technique to accommodate slower writing as well as transferring items from one set of bubbles to the center of more sets of bubbles.

Try these variations . . .
- Split the group into small teams (between two and five participants). Have each team complete a set of bubbles. Then share results with the whole group and follow steps 6 through 8 above.
- Split the group into small teams (between two and five participants). Have each team complete a set of bubbles. Have the teams swap bubble sets and then follow steps 6 through 8 above. Finish by having the teams share their results with the whole group.

(text continues on page 42)

FIGURE 4-1

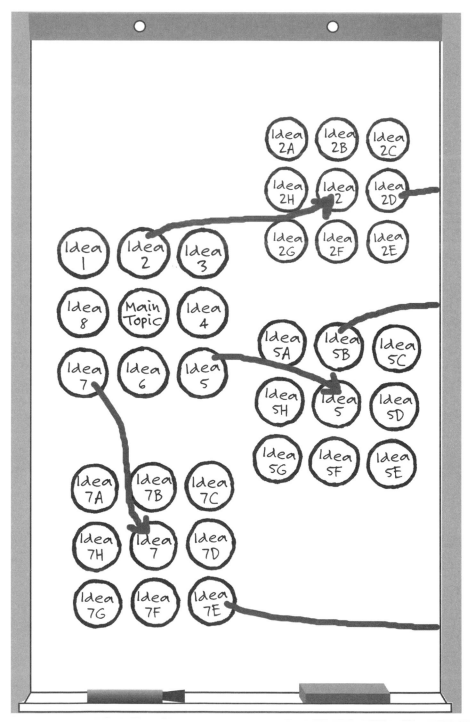

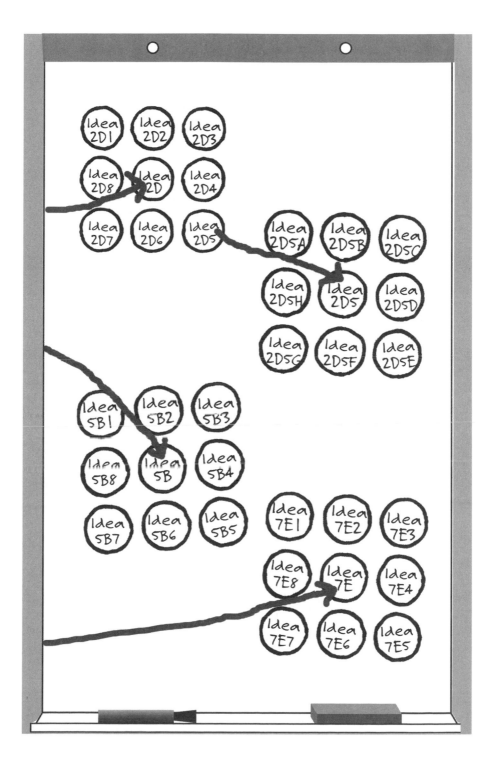

FIGURE 4-2

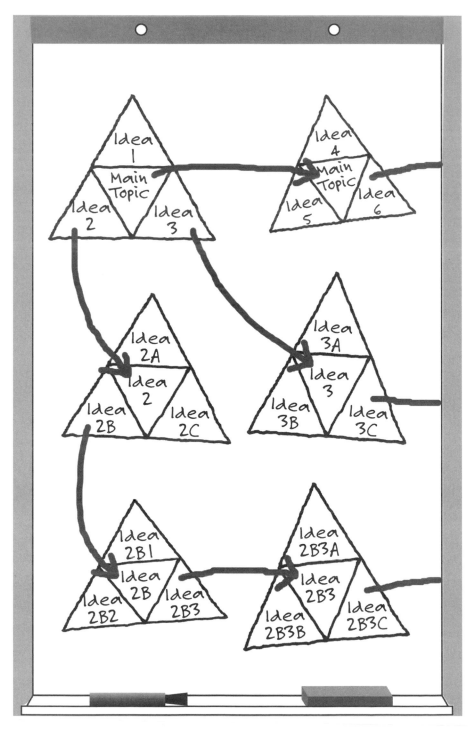

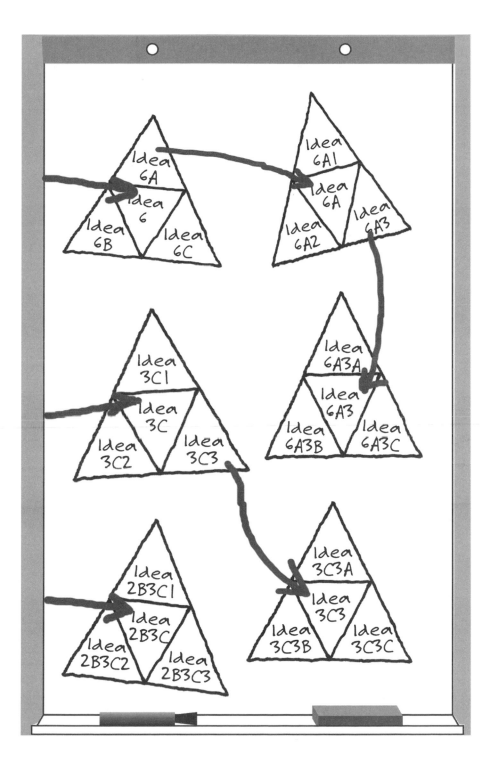

➤ Have participants individually complete a set of bubbles first. Then share results with the whole group and follow steps 6 through 8 above.
➤ Use triangles instead of bubbles. Put the topic in the middle triangle and record three responses in the surrounding triangles. Then put each of those three responses in the middle of new triangles. Figure 4–2 shows how this might work. Notice that the group did not deem all ideas equal, and that only ideas 2, 3, and 6 had traction.

CHIPS

This is . . .   ➤ A brainstorming technique that forces participants to come up with a specified number of ideas, instead of "as many as you can in this time period."

What it does . . .
➤ Puts the focus on individual responsibility as each participant must contribute the same number of ideas as everyone else.
➤ Helps neutralize some of the more dominant members of the group by limiting their participation.
➤ Adds an element of fun as participants toss chips into the bucket to represent their contributions.

One draw-back is . . .
➤ This activity may cause participants to feel too much pressure to come up with ideas when they feel that they have no more.

What you need . . .
➤ 10 chips (or coins, paper clips, or any other plentiful object) per participant.
➤ Bucket, box, or other large container to collect the chips as they are used.
➤ One board (flip chart, white board, etc.) and a marker.

Here's how . . .
1. Review the purpose of the session with the group.
2. Review and get agreement on the four rules of brainstorming (see Chapter 1).
3. Hand out 10 chips to each participant. The chips represent their answers to the Focus Question.
4. Explain that they should toss a chip into the bucket each time they give a response.

5. Ask the Focus Question.
6. Record their response as they toss their chip into the bucket.
7. End the session only after all participants have used all of their chips.
8. Sort or prioritize using the methods in Chapter 6 or 7.

Tips for success . . .
- This activity can work for any group size. With larger groups, however, give participants fewer chips, say five or six, or the activity will take too long.
- Be prepared for participants who finish early and want to help others get rid of their chips. You must declare at the start of the exercise whether this will be "legal."
- Go around the room and get one chip/response from each participant just to get things started. Then open it up for responses from anyone in any order. If the team stalls, go around the room again, soliciting one response from each participant.

Try these variations . . .
- Instead of distributing chips that participants work to eliminate, reward participants with a chip for each response. Perhaps declare how many chips must be collected by a participant. Or, at the end of the activity, allow them to exchange their earned chips for small prizes.
- Use pennies instead of chips. Each time a participant contributes an idea, he or she tosses two pennies into the bucket, representing their "two cents' worth."
- After participants have finished, give them each three more chips and ask them to push themselves, and come up with three more responses each!
- Put the participants in small teams (between two and four people) and give a stack of chips to each team. Instead of participants being individually responsible for getting rid of the chips, it's the team's responsibility. This takes the burden off the quieter

ones, but may allow dominant participants to take over.

- ► Make it a competition. See who can get rid of his or her chips first. The same contest may be used for teams.
- ► Speed things up by using time limits. Anyone who gets rid of all their chips within a time period gets a prize.
- ► Begin the session with participants standing. Allow them to sit only after they've gotten rid of a certain number of chips.
- ► Use dice instead of chips. Participants each throw a die. The number indicates how many responses they must give to the Focus Question.

GRIDS

This is . . . ▶ A brainstorming technique where participants use grids to prompt or guide their responses to a topic.

What it does . . . ▶ Helps a group that may have difficulty coming up with more than a small number of responses.
▶ Encourages and builds upon initial individual input.
▶ Keeps the group motivated to come up with more responses to fill the grids.

One drawback is . . . ▶ The amount of "structure" in this activity may inhibit some participants.

What you need . . . ▶ One board (flip chart, white board, etc.) and a marker.
▶ A stopwatch or timer.

Here's how . . . 1. Draw a grid on the board with the same number of rows and columns (between three and six of each).
2. Review the purpose of the session with the group.
3. Review and get agreement on the four rules of brainstorming (see Chapter 1).
4. Ask the Focus Question and start the clock.
5. Record each response in a column heading and simultaneously in a row heading. (Yes, you are filling these headings, across and down, with the same ideas.)
6. After the column and row headings are full, ask the participants to use the intersections of rows and columns to prompt more responses by combining or

comparing the things in the column and row headings.

7. Use more grids as appropriate. As structured in Figure 4–3, you will only be exploring four ideas and their combinations. You will probably want to do two, three, or even four individual grids in any given brainstorming session.

8. Sort or prioritize using the methods in Chapter 6 or 7.

Tips for success . . .

➤ The response that goes in the first column heading also goes in the first row heading. The response in the second column heading also goes in the second row heading, and so on.

➤ Each intersection in the grid is an opportunity for more responses. Column 1 plus Row 3, Column 1 plus Row 4, and so on.

➤ Even when the intersection is a duplicate (Column 2 with Row 2), the group may be inspired to find a new, creative response.

➤ The responses in the grid do not have to coincide nicely with the column and row headings. It's not about finding "right answers," it's about using the two-heading responses to spark more responses (whether the new responses are related or not) to the Focus Question.

Try these variations . . .

➤ Leave the row headings blank. Fill in the grid boxes with ideas prompted merely by the following column headings: "expand," "shrink," "deviate," and "combo" (or others of your choosing).

➤ Split the group into small teams. Have each team follow steps 1 through 5. Then swap grids and complete step 6.

➤ Create a grid with six columns. Label the columns: who, what, where, when, how, why. Ask the Focus Question. Participants use the column headings to generate responses.

➤ Use the variation above, except split the group into six teams. Ask the Focus Question and have each

FIGURE 4-3

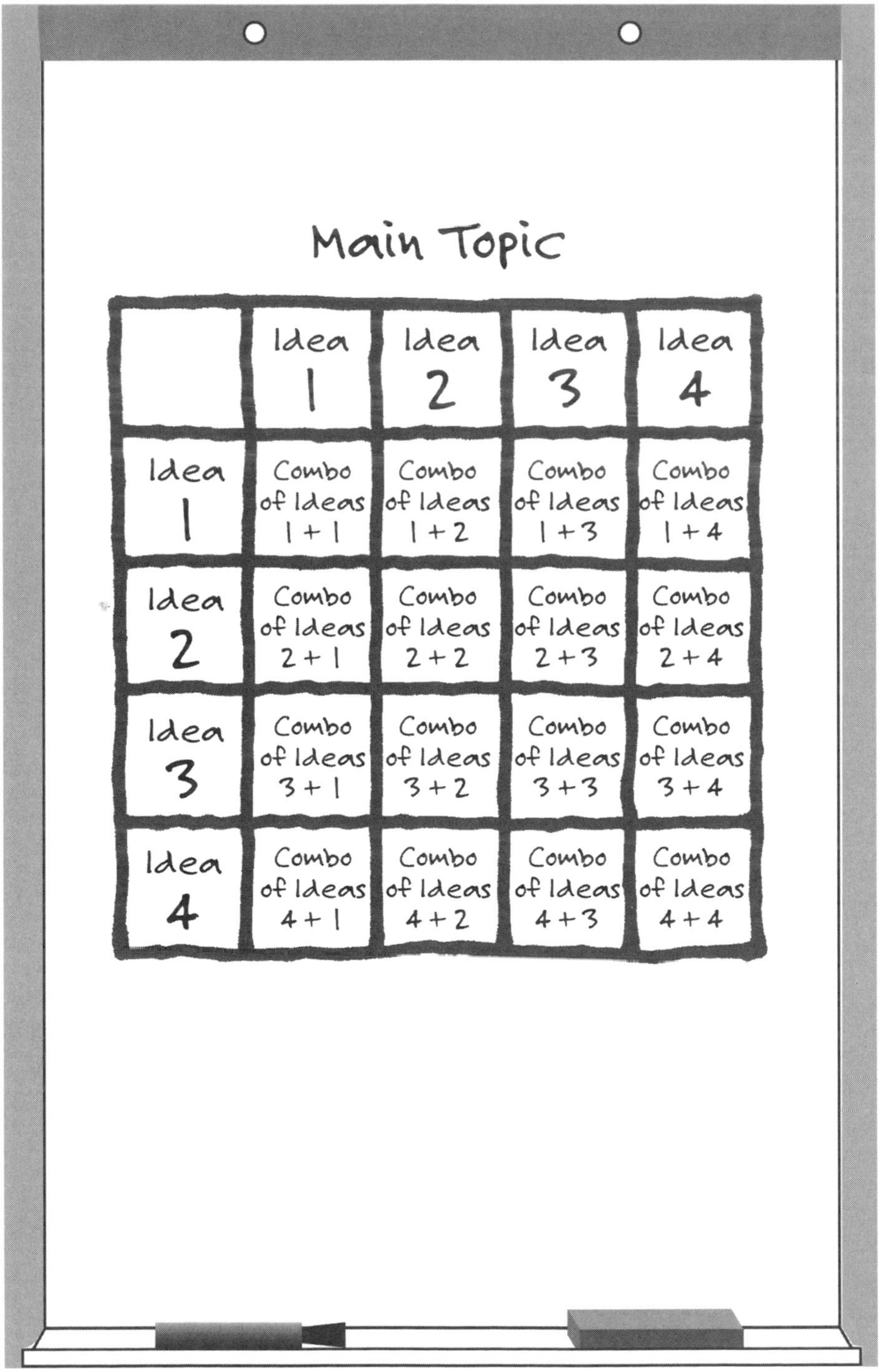

Main Topic

	Idea 1	Idea 2	Idea 3	Idea 4
Idea 1	Combo of Ideas 1 + 1	Combo of Ideas 1 + 2	Combo of Ideas 1 + 3	Combo of Ideas 1 + 4
Idea 2	Combo of Ideas 2 + 1	Combo of Ideas 2 + 2	Combo of Ideas 2 + 3	Combo of Ideas 2 + 4
Idea 3	Combo of Ideas 3 + 1	Combo of Ideas 3 + 2	Combo of Ideas 3 + 3	Combo of Ideas 3 + 4
Idea 4	Combo of Ideas 4 + 1	Combo of Ideas 4 + 2	Combo of Ideas 4 + 3	Combo of Ideas 4 + 4

team respond using one of the six column headings (who, what, where, when, how, why).

- ➤ Leave the row headings blank. Fill in the column headings with the first few responses from the participants. Then fill in the row headings with random words that are unrelated to the topic (dog, spatula, Ireland, lipstick, the year 1999, etc.) and follow the rest of the steps above.
- ➤ Write all the options on separate index cards. Shuffle the cards and draw two at random. Use this pairing to generate new ideas.

LAST ONE STANDING

This is . . .
- A brainstorming technique similar to the brainstorming activity Stickies but where teams compete with each other to generate the largest number of brainstorming responses.

What it does . . .
- Encourages participants to compete with each other for a larger quantity of brainstorming ideas.
- Allows all members of a large group to contribute because of small-group team approach.
- Raises the energy in the group because of the competition.

One drawback is . . .
- This activity misses the spontaneity and energy that comes from full group interaction.

What you need . . .
- Pads of large (3" x 5" or larger) stickies.
- A marker for each participant.
- A stopwatch or timer.
- Prizes for the winning team (optional).

Here's how . . .
1. Review the purpose of the session with the group.
2. Review and get agreement on the four rules of brainstorming (see Chapter 1).
3. Divide the group into as many small teams (between three and five participants) as necessary.
4. Distribute a marker and a pad of stickies to each team.
5. Explain that they will have 4 minutes to write on their stickies as many responses to the Focus Question as they can.

6. Explain that each separate response goes on its own separate sticky.
7. Have each team choose a Team Leader to record their ideas on the stickies.
8. When the teams are set, ask the Focus Question and start the clock.
9. When the time is up, the Team Leaders gather their team's stickies and get in line up front.
10. Team Leader #1 reads and posts his or her first sticky, and then goes to the back of the line.
11. Team Leader #2 does the same, and so on through all the Team Leaders.
12. Repeat this order until the last sticky is shared.
13. Any time the group feels a sticky is a duplicate of something already posted, they stand up and make a buzzer sound. If it is a duplicate, discard that sticky and send that Team Leader to the back of the line.
14. A second duplicate sticky eliminates that team.
15. If the Team Leader runs out of stickies, his or her team is eliminated.
16. The team with the last Team Leader standing wins. See Figure 4–4 for a flow chart of this activity.
17. Sort or prioritize using the methods in Chapter 6 or 7.

Tips for success . . .
- Using index cards and tape in place of sticky notes can work just fine.
- Give each team a different-colored pad of stickies. This will help keep track of when the second duplicate happens.
- Standing up and making a buzzer sound helps keep the participants engaged—and the energy high— while all the reading happens.

Try these variations . . .
- For small groups, don't divide into teams at all. Have each participant record their own ideas on stickies. Then they all get in line up front and follow the rest of the steps 10 through 17 above.
- Combine this activity with a grouping activity (see Chapter 6) to accomplish two things at once. As the Team Leader reads a sticky, he or she can post it into the appropriate category.

FIGURE 4-4

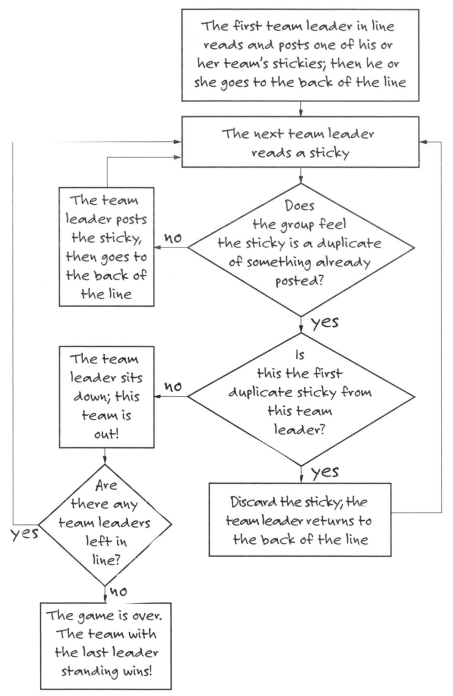

MIND MAPS

This is . . .   ➤ A brainstorming technique where participants' responses are recorded in visual graphics to promote more open, free-flowing ideas.

What it does . . .
➤ Encourages participants to build off of each other's input.
➤ Appeals to participants with a preference for making the input visual.
➤ Offers a more random, less linear approach.
➤ Helps participants see relationships and connections among their responses.

One draw-back is . . .
➤ This activity may be confusing or too fast-paced for some participants.

What you need . . .
➤ Large board (large butcher paper, multiple flip chart pages taped together, large white board, etc.).
➤ Marker(s).

Here's how . . .
1. Review the purpose of the session with the group.
2. Review and get agreement on the four rules of brainstorming (see Chapter 1).
3. Write the topic in a circle at the center of the board.
4. Draw a line in any direction coming out of the circle.
5. Ask the Focus Question and start the clock.
6. Record the first response on that line.
7. Each time a new, unique response is given, draw another line from the center to record that response.

See Figure 4–5 for an example of what this might look like.

8. If a response relates to, or builds upon, something already on the board, draw a line from that original item and record the additional response.
9. Sort or prioritize using the methods in Chapter 6 or 7.

Tips for success . . .

➤ Don't worry about making the lines horizontal. Drawing spokes will help you make full use of the large board.

➤ Don't worry about the Mind Map being orderly and balanced or centered on the large board. Some ideas may generate more activity than others, and weigh down the Mind Map in one section of the large board. If this happens, just draw long lines from that area to an empty area and keep going.

➤ Give more time to this technique to allow for the drawing and writing.

Try these variations . . .

➤ Split the group into smaller teams and have them each create a Mind Map. Have the teams share their responses with the whole group. After all have shared, be sure to gather any more responses the participants may have created based on what they just heard!

➤ Have participants each create their own Mind Map. Put them in pairs or small groups to share their work with each other. Have them consolidate their Mind Maps before sharing with the whole group.

➤ Draw a certain number of lines from the center topic. Encourage the group to come up with a response for each line before building on any of them.

FIGURE 4-5

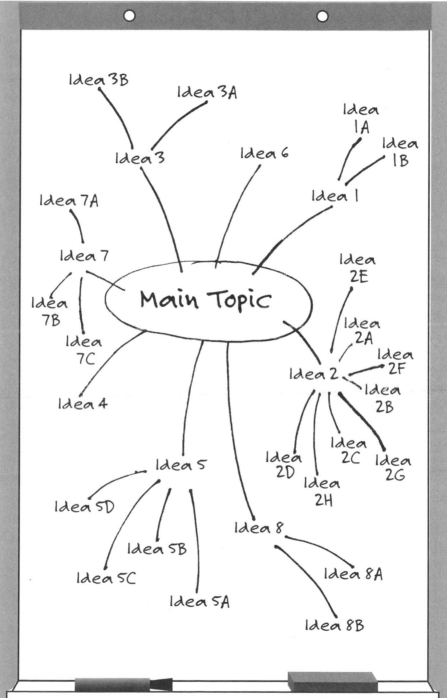

PAPER SWAP

This is . . .
- A brainstorming technique where participants write their input on separate pieces of paper; then they swap papers and continue to add input.

What it does . . .
- Gives everyone a chance to participate.
- Keeps input almost anonymous.
- Minimizes the tendency to critique or judge input.

Drawbacks are . . .
- This activity misses the spontaneity and energy that comes from full group interaction.
- It also requires that someone (you?) spend a great deal of time "consolidating" the responses once everyone has made their contribution.

What you need . . .
- At least one sheet of paper (preferably lined) per participant.
- Pen or pencil per participant.
- A stopwatch or timer.

Here's how . . .
1. Review the purpose of the session with the group.
2. Review and get agreement on the four rules of brainstorming (see Chapter 1).
3. Distribute a pen and a piece of paper to each participant.
4. Explain that the session will consist of several short rounds.
5. At the start of each round, you will ask the Focus Question, and then start the clock for 30 to 60 seconds.
6. Participants independently write their responses (legibly!) on their own papers.

7. When time is up, participants turn their paper face down and swap repeatedly and quickly with anyone nearby. Each time they get another paper, swap it again with someone else until you tell them to stop (give them about 10 seconds to do this—just enough to be sure the papers are well shuffled).

8. When "shuffle time" is up, each person turns over the paper in hand and picks up their pen.

9. Ask the Focus Question again and restart the clock. (Don't do this *each* time, of course, or participants may start rolling their eyes.)

10. Participants may add more original input below what is already on the paper.

11. Participants may also read what is on the paper and then combine or build upon those ideas to create new ones.

12. Repeat the rounds until the energy wanes. A final page might look something like the one in Figure 4–6.

13. Consolidate the input and post it for all to see. You may want to do this while the participants take a break, or have one or more of them help you.

14. Sort or prioritize using the methods in Chapter 6 or 7.

Tips for success . . .

► Although this activity works well with any size group, the larger the group, the greater the task of consolidating the input from all the papers.

► Make the rounds shorter if you anticipate their responses to be a word or two (where should we hold the company picnic this year?) and longer if you expect their responses to be a sentence or two (how can we improve our hiring process?).

► Encourage them to write legibly.

► The more rounds you have, the longer it takes for a participant to read what was already written, so extend the time after the first few rounds.

► It's okay for participants to write the same idea on more than one paper—especially if they get stuck and can't think of anything new. In larger groups, often a participant won't see that idea from the first

FIGURE 4-6

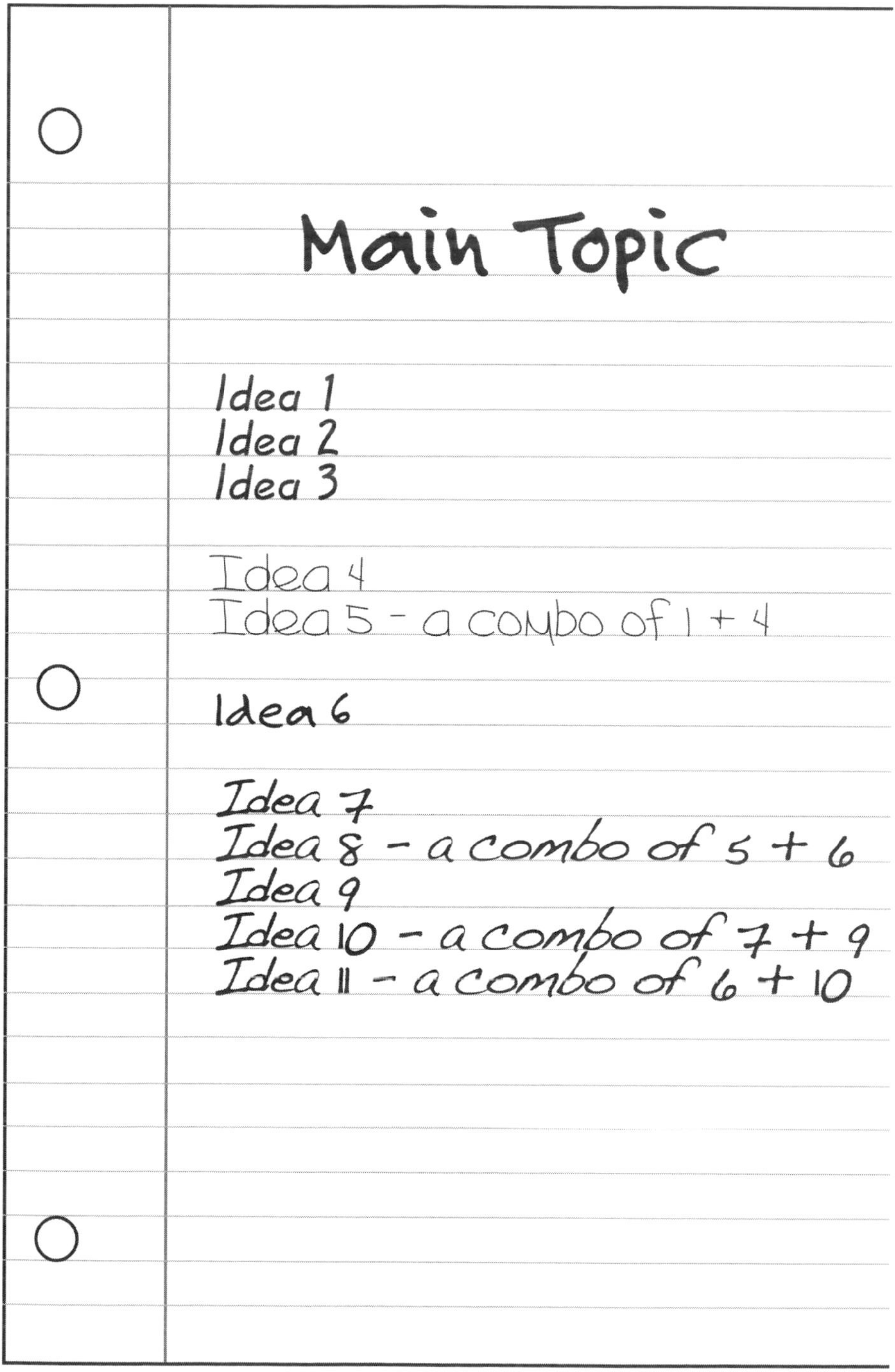

Main Topic

Idea 1
Idea 2
Idea 3

Idea 4
Idea 5 – a combo of 1 + 4

Idea 6

Idea 7
Idea 8 – a combo of 5 + 6
Idea 9
Idea 10 – a combo of 7 + 9
Idea 11 – a combo of 6 + 10

paper, but may see it on the second, and come up with something else. Encourage them not to just keep writing the same thing over and over, though.

➤ It's okay if the whole idea doesn't get written before the time is up. Perhaps the fragment of an idea may inspire the next person's brainstorming.

➤ Expect some participants to be mildly flustered with the quick pace, particularly the first round or two. This is because they want to write all their ideas at once. Remind them that there will be many rounds, many opportunities to get all of their ideas included.

Try these variations . . .

➤ Vary the length of the rounds—make some 15–20 seconds long, others 60, 90, or even 120 seconds. Be careful that the rounds are not so long that participants have too much downtime.

➤ Structure the paper swapping. Put participants in a circle. Each round, they pass their paper to the person on their left.

➤ On even-numbered rounds (or every third or fourth round), do not allow any new, out-of-the-blue ideas. Instead, insist that the ideas for that round be derived from what is already written on the paper.

➤ Instead of time limits, ask each participant to write two or three ideas. Tell them that as soon as they are done with that many, they should find someone else who is also done and swap. Don't wait for a signal, just swap. And then write two or three more ideas—and swap again with whoever else is ready to swap. There is no taking turns. This variation works best with larger groups (over 10). With smaller groups, participants will often have to wait for someone else to finish their input so they can swap.

➤ Have participants pair up. After round one, they swap papers only with their partners. After round two, they swap back. After round three, they find a new partner and repeat. The tendency will be to talk rather than write, so encourage them (for now) to stay silent and write.

PLUS ONE

This is . . .
➤ A brainstorming technique where participants add their input one at a time, but without prior knowledge of each other's input.

What it does . . .
➤ Helps neutralize some of the more dominant members of the group.
➤ Gives everyone a chance to share their own input fully.
➤ Helps participants feel heard and understood completely when it's their turn to give input.

Drawbacks are . . .
➤ This activity slows down the brainstorming, as this method is iterative.
➤ It also lacks the spontaneity and energy that comes from full group interaction—at least until the very end.

What you need . . .
➤ One board (flip chart, white board, etc.) and a marker.

Here's how . . .
1. In advance, review the purpose of the session with the group.
2. Review and get agreement on the four rules of brainstorming (see Chapter 1).
3. Ask the Focus Question and request that they contemplate their responses as they await their turn.
4. Begin the session with only two participants in the room.
5. Have them share their ideas with each other (record them on the board).

6. Add one participant, seated so he or she cannot see the board of ideas yet.

7. That participant shares his or her ideas (add them to the board).

8. Then share the original pair's input with that new participant.

9. Ask all three to add any new ideas they now have, given the input that was just added.

10. Invite another participant into the room and do the same.

11. Repeat steps 6 through 10 until all participants have been incorporated into the process.

12. Sort or prioritize using the methods in Chapter 6 or 7.

Tips for success . . .

► This activity works best for small groups (fewer than 10). Any larger, and the participants get overwhelmed. They may tire out if they participate early, or get bored waiting to participate if they are at the end of the process.

► Since the first few participants in the process will spend the most time and energy, choose those who are most vested or most passionate about the topic.

► This activity is ideal for neutralizing dominant participants. Place them later in the process. Place quieter or less confident participants earlier in the process.

► Give the participants waiting to enter the room something to do to keep them from discussing the topic ahead of time or getting bored. You may even want to stagger their "start time" for when they are to show up to join the session.

► Ensure that the group is especially mindful of the "no critiquing" rule while they are listening to the new participant share his or her input. They should listen quietly and respectfully until that participant is finished. Post the four rules of brainstorming as a reminder.

> ➤ This activity works well with virtual brainstorming. Each participant joins the session by connecting at his or her designated time.

Try these variations . . .

> ➤ Have the whole group start at the same time. Participants pair up. Share and record their input. (You will need several flip charts and markers if you do this variation.) Each pair then combines with another pair to create a quartet. Share input and build on the ideas to create new ones. The quartets disband. Each pair then finds a new pair to create a new quartet. Repeat as desired. Have each group report their ideas to the whole group.

> ➤ For large groups, use the variation above (including the extra boards), but begin with participants in trios. Combine the trios into sextets.

> ➤ Split the group into half. Using two boards, conduct the activity concurrently for both halves as described above. Finally, combine the two halves and have them share their ideas with each other, building on what they hear for even more ideas.

ROUND ROBIN

This is . . .
> A brainstorming technique where participants will move from board to board as they brainstorm different issues at the same time.

What it does . . .
> Allows the group to brainstorm several topics at once.
> Engages the participants with a fast pace and physical movement.
> Offers change and variety throughout even the shortest brainstorming session.
> Sparks creativity as participants move from topic to topic and their brains shift to keep up.

On drawback is . . .
> Some participants may become distracted or disoriented as they move from topic to topic in rapid succession.

What you need . . .
> One board (flip chart, white board, etc.) per topic to be brainstormed.
> One marker per board.
> A stopwatch or timer.

Here's how . . .
1. Space the boards equidistant around the room.
2. Label each board with a different topic.
3. Review the purpose of the session with the group.
4. Review and get agreement on the four rules of brainstorming (see Chapter 1).
5. Divide the group so that there are roughly the same number of participants at each board; one participant will be scribe for each team.

6. Ask the Focus Questions relevant to each board. Tell the participants to listen to all of the Focus Questions, but to pay special attention to the one for their board. Then, start the clock for 3 minutes so the groups can begin to brainstorm.
7. When time is up, all brainstorming must stop.
8. The scribe stays at the board, while the rest of the participants move to the next board (see Figure 4–7).
9. Restart the timer. Scribes remind the new participants of the topic and prompt brainstorming.
10. When time is up, all brainstorming must stop.
11. The scribe gives the marker to someone at that board. That new scribe stays while the rest of the participants, including the prior scribe, move to the next board.
12. Repeat steps 11 through 13 for as many boards as there are.
13. Sort or prioritize using the methods in Chapter 6 or 7.

Tips for success . . .
- ▸ This activity can work well when the group is too large to brainstorm all together.
- ▸ This activity works best with between three and six topics/boards. Fewer than three, and it feels forced. More than six, and it becomes overwhelming for the participants.
- ▸ Charge each scribe to vigilantly enforce the "no critiquing" rule at each board.
- ▸ Anyone who is a scribe will not make it to all of the boards. After the Round Robin, open each board for 60 seconds for "any last thoughts" to include any ideas from those who didn't make it to that board.
- ▸ Number the boards to make the movement to the next one easier. For example, the participants from board #1 will go to board #2, from #2 go to #3, and so on.

Try these variations . . .
- ▸ Each board doesn't have to be different. For example, you may have two topics but use six boards. Every

FIGURE 4-7

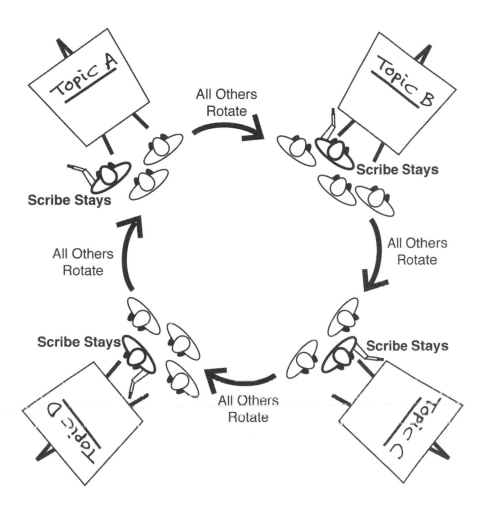

other board is the same topic. Each group will brainstorm differently at their boards. When participants come to a board with a topic they've already done, that board may prompt more, different ideas to record.

➤ Use the above variation for just one topic. Each board is the same. The small teams brainstorm at a board and then move to the next board. The topic is the same, but they can read what was written by the last team and that may spark more ideas.

➤ Run the activity only for two or three rounds. Then gather the entire group back together and brainstorm each board again as a large group (adding to, or building upon, the initial list started by the smaller groups in the Round Robin).

➤ Have the scribes stay at the same board throughout the activity. Scribes may volunteer to stay at a board they are particularly passionate about. They need to stay especially mindful of the "no critiquing" rule of brainstorming.

➤ Instead of forcing participants to move together to the next board, allow them to individually move to whatever board they choose. This will mix up the groups more and allow participants to go to where their energy or passion lies.

➤ Have the role of scribe at the board change as each idea is given. After one participant gives an idea and the scribe records it, he or she hands the marker to another participant. When time is called, whoever has the marker is the one who stays at that board while the others move to the next one.

SILENT BRAINSTORM

This is . . .   ► A brainstorming technique where participants simultaneously write their brainstorm ideas on a board without speaking.

What it does . . .
- ► Gives everyone a chance to participate.
- ► Minimizes the tendency to critique or judge input.
- ► Engages the participants physically.

One draw-back is . . .   ► This activity slows down the brainstorming because it takes more time to write than to speak.

What you need . . .
- ► Large writing surface (several flip chart pages posted; very long white board; long piece of butcher paper).
- ► One marker for each participant.
- ► A stopwatch or timer.

Here's how . . .
1. Review the purpose of the session with the group.
2. Review and get agreement on the four rules of brainstorming (see Chapter 1).
3. Explain that the brainstorming will be conducted in complete silence. Once the Focus Question is asked, participants may not speak.
4. Distribute one marker to each participant.
5. Ask the Focus Question and start the clock.
6. Participants write as many responses as they can (legibly!) on the board in the time given (5 minutes is reasonable).
7. Sort or prioritize using the methods in Chapter 6 or 7.

Tips for success...

- This activity works best with smaller groups (up to 10); the larger the group, the larger the writing surface needs to be so all participants can be actively writing at the same time.
- Encourage participants to read what others have written and use those ideas to prompt their own newer ones.
- Encourage participants to limit their written responses (fewer than three words? fewer than seven words?) so time and energy aren't lost unnecessarily.
- Expect some participants to be frustrated with writing legibly or spelling properly. Remind them to focus on their great responses, and not to worry about spelling, grammar, or other less important factors of the exercise.
- This activity works well for virtual teams. After steps 1, 2, 3, and 5 above, participants input their responses to the virtual bulletin board.

Try these variations . . .

- Have participants exchange markers (for different colors) after each response they give. This will help mask which responses are by the same participant.
- Challenge them all to be able to use all of the colors provided as a fun way to promote greater quantity.
- Line participants in a single file. Use one marker. The first person in line runs to the board and writes his or her response. They hand the marker to the next person in line, and then they rejoin the line at the back. The next person writes their response on the board, and so on. The focus is on a frantic speed. While waiting in line, participants can be forming more ideas based on what they see being written.
- Use the above variation, but vary the time randomly without telling participants what their personal time limit will be when they begin. Thirty seconds for one, 20 for another, 45 for the next.
- Use the variation above except put the participants in two or more lines. Have the lines compete with

each other to see which one can run through all of their participants first. See Figure 4–8.

► Use the above variations, but intead of limiting each participant to one idea at a time, limit them to 20 or 30 seconds. If they can get multiple responses on the board, all the better! When time is up, the next person literally takes the pen from the other participant (even if he or she is in the middle of writing a word!). This can be fun, but also can be disruptive for some.

► Use two large boards and do the original activity, or any of the variations above in teams where a small prize is awarded to the team that generates the most responses.

► Rather than writing words, have participants draw pictures to represent their responses. After a specific time period, allow them to ask each other to clarify pictures that may not be obvious. Then declare silent time again and let them draw more responses. Repeat as necessary.

FIGURE 4-8

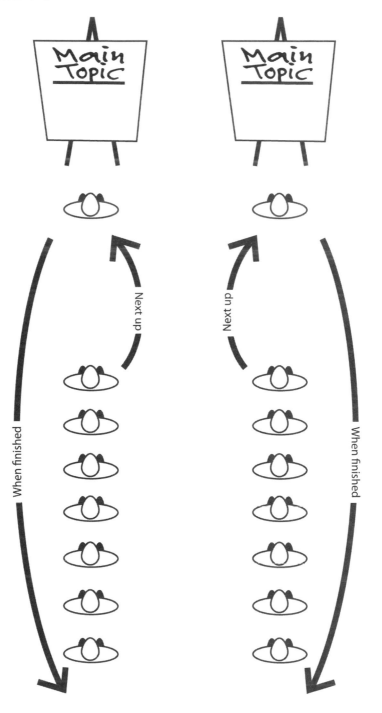

TAKING TURNS

This is . . .
- A brainstorming technique where all of the participants take turns responding to the Focus Question in order.

What it does . . .
- Gives everyone a chance to participate.
- Helps neutralize some of the more dominant members of the group.
- Slows the process down so participants can build off of each other's input.

One drawback is . . .
- This activity may go so slowly that the session stalls.

What you need . . .
- One board (flip chart, white board, etc.) and a marker.
- A stopwatch or timer.

Here's how . . .
1. Review the purpose of the session with the group.
2. Review and get agreement on the four rules of brainstorming (see Chapter 1).
3. Determine how long you want the activity to run. Perhaps as little as 10 minutes, or as long as 20 or more. The larger the group, the more time you'll want to allow.
4. Explain that everyone will get a turn to contribute in order, and that at each turn they will have 30 seconds to offer as many ideas as they can.
5. Indicate who will give the first response, and what the order will be (around the circle, from left to right, etc.).

6. Ask the Focus Question and start the clock.
7. Record the first participant's response and move to the next one.
8. Any participant may pass if they don't have a response ready.
9. Repeat until time is up.
10. Sort or prioritize using the methods in Chapter 6 or 7.

Tips for success . . .

► Encourage participants to pass if they don't have a response ready immediately. The session will move quicker that way, keeping the energy high. And, they will get another chance to contribute in a few moments when their turn comes up again.

► Don't let participants rush or pressure those who may not have an input on their turn. After hearing a few more responses, they may then have something relevant to contribute.

► Follow the order outlined. If you make exceptions to the order, you risk losing credibility or objectivity with the group.

► After everyone has had a turn, shorten the time to 20 seconds. This will keep the session moving even after everyone's initial burst of ideas.

Try these variations . . .

► Rather than just going around the room, set up the participants in order alphabetically by first name; chronologically by birthday; or some other simple, fun method.

► Number index cards 1 through as many as there are participants. Participants randomly draw a card with a number on it. The order to follow is indicated by the numbers on their cards. Or, use playing cards.

► Give one participant a bean bag. After they have responded, they toss it to someone else, who is now given the option of contributing. After the second person responds (or passes), they toss the bean bag to someone else. The goal is to keep the bean bag moving quickly among all the participants, but not in a set order.

- ► Use the variation above, except have the participant toss the bean bag *before* he or she begins to share their input. That way, the one who just received the bean bag has a moment to collect his or her thoughts before needing to respond.
- ► Use dice. After (or before) the participant responds, he or she will toss the dice to get a number. The next participant is the one who is that many seats away from the one who tossed the dice.
- ► Use the variation above, but replace dice with a deck of cards well shuffled and missing the face cards. After (or before) the participant responds, draw a card to reveal a number. The next participant is the one who is that many seats away from the one who drew the card.

CHAPTER 5

CREATIVITY EXERCISES

U se these activities to spark and encourage even greater creativity in your brainstorming session. Combine one of these exercises with a brainstorming technique in Chapter 4 to give the brainstorming session structure.

The materials listed for each of these activities are for that specific activity only. When you combine an activity from this chapter with one from Chapter 4, be sure to secure the materials listed for that activity as well.

ASSOCIATIONS

This is . . .   ➤ A creativity exercise where participants get brain-storming inspiration by forcing an association between the topic and some random, unrelated concept.

What it does . . .   ➤ Adds interesting fun (through random concepts) to the brainstorming.
➤ Gets participants into a different mindset that will inspire different perspectives.

One draw-back is . . .   ➤ Participants may get distracted by the many random thoughts provided.

What you need . . .   ➤ One slip of paper per participant.
➤ One pen per participant.

Here's how . . .   1. Select and prepare to use a brainstorming technique from Chapter 4.
2. Review the purpose of the session with the group.
3. Review and get agreement on the four rules of brain-storming (see Chapter 1).
4. Have the participants write one random noun (including places or people—real or make-believe) on a slip of paper, then fold it in half.
5. Have them exchange the slips randomly with each other repeatedly until you tell them to stop and open the slip in their hands.
6. Explain that their challenge is to associate the nouns on their papers to the Focus Question.

7. Ask the Focus Question and start the clock (5–15 minutes is reasonable; remember, you don't want to burn them out).
8. Brainstorm, using the technique you selected.
9. Sort or prioritize using the methods in Chapter 6 or 7.

For example . . .

► Participants may write any noun. Use objects (a speck of dust, a cheetah, plastic, a rose thorn); concepts (the theory of relativity, a dream, wedding jitters); people dead or alive, real or fictional (Cleopatra, Peter Pan, a grandparent, Obama, Lucille Ball, Mother Theresa); an event (Halloween, high school graduation, weightlifting, the Great Depression) or a place (the Grand Canyon, Japan, under the bed, Mars, in a Petri dish).

Tips for success . . .

► Depending on the brainstorming technique used, this exercise can work with any group size.

► After some brainstorming, have the participants swap their slips again for more inspiration. Or, tell them to initiate swapping their slip of paper with another participant whenever theirs doesn't inspire them anymore.

► Use the hundreds of ready-made noun cards in Mattel's Apples-to-Apples® board game.

Try these variations . . .

► Use more than one slip of paper for each participant. When they've finished writing their nouns, have them put the slips in a cardboard box or paper bag. Then have each participant reach in and select two or three slips of paper. When they're "tapped out," they can return their slips to the box and collect new ones.

► Rather than nouns, provide slips of paper with random rules or instructions that will force some kind of connection to the topic. For example, "rinse, lather, repeat" or "refrigerate after opening." Ask, "How can we connect our Topic X to the rule on your slip of paper?" A response may be, "My slip says 'refrigerate after opening' so I'm wondering if we should add some kind of cooling-off period to the process."

► Rather than nouns, provide slips of paper with random phrases that participants will force into some kind of analogy. For example, "swimming against the tide" or "peeling a banana." Ask, "How is our Topic X like what's written on your slip of paper?" A response would start, "Well, Topic X is like peeling a banana in that . . ."

BRAINSTORM BASH

This is . . .
- A highly competitive, creative exercise where participants compete in teams with each other to think up the most creative ideas.

What it does . . .
- Adds an element of competition to encourage more creativity.
- Raises the energy in the group.

One drawback is . . .
- This activity purposefully violates the "no critiquing" rule of brainstorming for the benefit of adding competitive pressure.

What you need . . .
- One board (flip chart, white board, etc.) and a marker.
- A stopwatch or timer.
- Prizes for the winning team (optional).

Here's how . . .
1. Divide the group into three or more teams of roughly the same size.
2. Share with the group the objective of the session, or ask a Focus Question.
3. Randomly select one team to go first. They have 60 seconds to propose the most crazy, outlandish, ridiculous solution that they can think of.
4. The other teams then have 3 minutes to develop a truly feasible solution based on the first team's original idea.
5. All teams present their solutions and the first team chooses the best, most plausible solution.
6. Record *all* the ideas.

7. The winning team then has 60 seconds to propose yet another crazy, outlandish, ridiculous solution.
8. Repeat steps 6 through 8 several times.
9. Award a prize to the team with the most points.
10. Sort or prioritize using the methods in Chapter 6 or 7.

Tips for success . . .

- ➤ This exercise can work with groups of fewer than 20 participants.
- ➤ Keep teams small. Larger teams will take more time to process their ideas and slow down the process, or some participants will be marginalized in the interest of being quick. Teams of between two and four participants are best.
- ➤ The goal remains lots of ideas, albeit feasible ones. Keep this game moving quickly. Encourage the judging team to decide the winners quickly!

Try these variations . . .

- ➤ Shorten (or lengthen) the time limits given in steps 5 or 6.
- ➤ For more distinction in judging, have the judging team select the winners, but give half a point to the idea they like second best.
- ➤ Conduct a quick session with everyone contributing ideas in step 5, instead of doing it in teams. Randomly choose one idea from that list and have all teams do step 6. All participants vote on the best idea presented—no one can vote for the idea that came from their team. Repeat.

MEGA-DOODLES

This is . . .
➤ A creativity exercise where participants create a group mega-doodle from which they gain inspiration about the topic.

What it does . . .
➤ Gives everyone a chance to contribute without having to be "artistic."
➤ Provides colorful visual stimulation for brainstorming.
➤ Adds some physical movement for participants as they mill around the board and doodle.

One drawback is . . .
➤ Some participants may feel intimidated by others who they think draw well, or doodle better than they do.

What you need . . .
➤ Large writing surface (several flip chart pages posted; large white board; long piece of butcher paper).
➤ At least one marker for each participant.

Here's how . . .
1. Select and prepare to use a brainstorming technique from Chapter 4.
2. Review the purpose of the session with the group.
3. Review and get agreement on the four rules of brainstorming (see Chapter 1).
4. Encourage the participants to doodle anywhere on the board and start the timer for 4 minutes (or less). Stress that they are not drawing pictures, just making doodles.

5. Ask them to move to another place at the board after they've drawn a doodle or two, and draw another, or add something to someone else's doodle.
6. Have them exchange markers frequently; encourage them to play with different colors and marker thicknesses.
7. Participants move about as often as they like, and whenever they like; there is no order or structure to when, where, or how they doodle.
8. When time is up, participants step back and admire the mega-doodle they have collectively drawn.
9. Encourage them to draw inspiration from the mega-doodle when you brainstorm.
10. Ask the Focus Question and start the clock.
11. Brainstorm, using the technique you selected.
12. Sort or prioritize using the methods in Chapter 6 or 7.

Tips for success . . .

► This exercise works well with any size group as long as there is plenty of board space so all participants can be doodling at the same time.

► Err on the side of too much, rather than too little, board space. There should be enough space that everyone can doodle at the same time and still have some space left over (so participants don't have to wait for someone to move in order to move themselves).

► Provide as many different-colored markers as possible. Markers of varying thicknesses are also good.

► Encourage all sorts of doodles. The goal is to fill the board. A larger doodle will usually provide greater inspiration than a smaller one.

► Remind participants to doodle, not draw, and move from place to place at the board. The goal is not to draw a picture or make anything structured, coherent, or planned. Random marks and lines are encouraged. As in brainstorming, there is no right or wrong doodle. Any doodle is welcome.

► For smaller groups, place the writing surface in the middle of a table that everyone can gather around and doodle on. Smaller markers, pens, and pencils can work. Rotate the chart frequently.

► Post separate charts around the room. Each chart will be a separate doodle that participants can add to at will. When brainstorming, each chart may be viewed differently and cause different creative thoughts.

► Have the participants join to make a "progressive doodle," with each member adding to a doodle in turn (see Figure 5–1). Make sure they each have a different-colored marker.

(text continues on page 86)

FIGURE 5-1

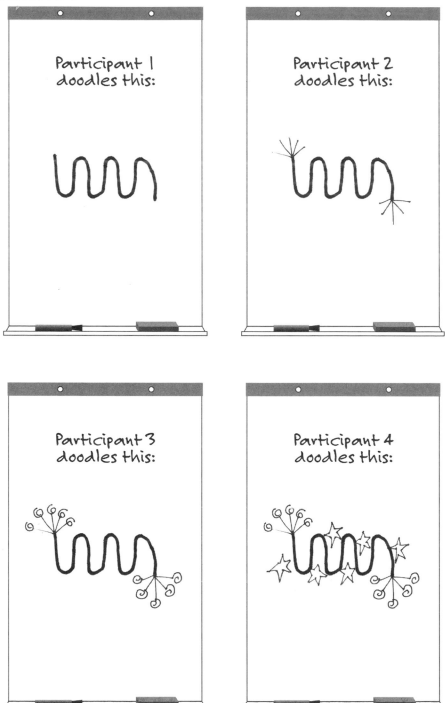

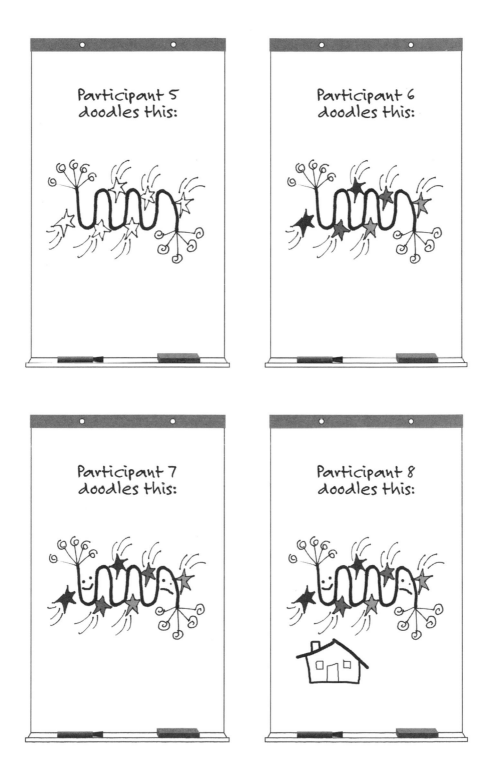

EXAGGERATIONS

This is . . .
- A creativity exercise where participants explore an exaggerated aspect of the topic.

What it does . . .
- Minimizes the tendency to critique or judge input.
- Encourages and builds upon initial individual input.

One drawback is . . .
- This activity can frustrate the more "realistic thinking" participants, who may object to playing with concepts so obviously impossible.

What you need . . .
- One board (flip chart, white board, etc.) and a marker.
- A stopwatch or timer.

Here's how . . .
1. Select and prepare to use a brainstorming technique from Chapter 4.
2. Take the topic, goal, or purpose of the brainstorming session and exaggerate it considerably.
3. Create a Focus Question for that exaggerated objective.
4. Review the purpose of the session with the group.
5. Review and get agreement on the four rules of brainstorming (see Chapter 1).
6. Ask the Focus Question and start the clock.
7. Brainstorm, using the technique you selected.
8. Sort or prioritize using the methods in Chapter 6 or 7.

For example . . .	► If the goal is to improve customer service scores from 88 to 90 (on a scale of 1–100), exaggerate it to 110.
	► If the goal is to reduce the time it takes to process an expense reimbursement from 21 days to 17 days, exaggerate it to 1 day.
Tips for success . . .	► Depending on the brainstorming technique used, this exercise can work with any group size.
	► Help the participants to have fun with the fantasy of the extreme or exaggerated. Remind them to remain playful and open themselves to the wild and absurd (lead by example here).
	► Exaggerate your own exaggerated version of the Focus Question. The goal is to be way, way out of touch with reality (briefly).
Try these variations . . .	► After an initial, more traditional brainstorming session, review each idea and do a mini-brainstorm: how could we make this response bigger/smaller; faster/slower; more/less expensive; etc.?
	► Conduct a more traditional brainstorming session. Have participants write down their favorite idea on the list. Then, have participants rip up that idea. Write a new one that exaggerates (bigger, better, faster, cheaper, etc.) the one they just ripped up. Share the new exaggerated/improved ideas with the group.
	► Play with the opposite of the exaggerated state. Go for the tiniest incremental change instead. How can we improve customer service scores by only 1/100th of one percent but no more? Then blow up those responses into exaggerated possibilities.
	► Conduct a more traditional brainstorming session. Revisit the list created from the perspective of 10 or even 100 years from now; from a different universe or plane of existence; from a dramatically different financial position; etc.

FORCED CONFLICT

This is . . .	► A creativity exercise where participants find inspiration for a seemingly dichotomous situation.
What it does . . .	► Gets participants into a different mindset that will inspire different perspectives. ► Encourages and builds upon initial individual input.
One drawback is . . .	► Some participants may have difficulty in putting conflicting concepts together.
What you need . . .	► No additional material.
Here's how . . .	1. Select and prepare to use a brainstorming technique from Chapter 4. 2. From the topic, find an essential element where there is some form of conflict. Frame the Focus Question around that conflict before the session. 3. Review the purpose of the session with the group. 4. Review and get agreement on the four rules of brainstorming (see Chapter 1). 5. Ask the Focus Question and start the clock. 6. Brainstorm, using the technique you selected. 7. Sort or prioritize using the methods in Chapter 6 or 7.
For example . . .	► If the topic is about improving customer service, one element might be dealing with customers who com-

plain. The goal is to turn them into happy customers. Create a Focus Question about how you can create "happy complainers."

➤ If the topic is about improving employee development efforts, one element is the fear of losing employees in whom you've invested. Create a Focus Question about how you can "create employees that headhunters can't resist."

Tips for
success . . .
➤ Depending on the brainstorming technique used, this exercise can work with any group size.

Try these
variations . . .
➤ You can combine this creative exercise with any other creativity exercises in this chapter for double benefit.

FREE WRITING

This is . . .
➤ A creativity exercise where participants gain brainstorming inspiration from independent writing.

What it does . . .
➤ Engages the participants physically (as they write).
➤ Allows participants to consider ideas before having to speak.
➤ Encourages participants to write their extremely wild ideas without fear of being judged or criticized.

One drawback is . . .
➤ Even though they only have to write (nonstop!) for 4 minutes, some participants may find this extremely difficult.

What you need . . .
➤ Paper and a pen for each participant.
➤ A stopwatch or timer.

Here's how . . .
1. Select and prepare to use a brainstorming technique from Chapter 4.
2. Review the purpose of the session with the group.
3. Review and get agreement on the four rules of brainstorming (see Chapter 1).
4. Tell participants that they are to write nonstop for 4 minutes once the Focus Question is asked.
5. Ask the Focus Question and start the clock.
6. Participants must begin to write immediately—ideally answering the question, but if they cannot, then they must write something, anything.
7. After 4 minutes, tell them to stop writing, and begin the brainstorming technique you selected. Their

writing may (or may not!) have prompted lots of ideas to share.

8. Sort or prioritize using the methods in Chapter 6 or 7.

For example . . .

➤ One participant's writing may look like this:

So I'm not sure what to write but she said I had to write and keep writing. She wants us to think of ways to improve the invoice system but I don't even use that system very much so I'm not sure why she or anyone else thinks I would have any ideas about how to improve that system. So I'm sitting here writing only because she keeps telling us to not stop writing, even if we are writing nothing, which is exactly what I'm doing, so I'm not being very productive. This is silly! I'm still writing and writing because she won't let me stop writing and if I do stop, she's going to tell me to keep writing, so I keep writing! I only hope Logan and Amanda are being more articulate, since they are the ones that use this system the most. I mean, they don't have any problems with it because they know it so well, they could do it with their eyes closed. If only I had half their experience, I'd be able to run things through a lot quicker, and nothing would get kicked back. And isn't that a pain! So I wonder if there's a way that I could instantly know it better . . . maybe that's what I'm supposed to be thinking about. But I don't have any ideas except do a brain transfer from Logan or Amanda directly to me. And if we can't do that, well, maybe they could just give us a cheat sheet on some of the ins and outs of the system so it's easier for those of us who only use it occasionally, to be able to navigate our way through it better . . .

➤ In the brainstorming session, perhaps this participant volunteers these ideas: a system cheat sheet, better training on the system, screens that are easier to navigate.

Tips for success . . .	▶ This exercise works well with groups of any size.
	▶ State up front—and constantly remind them throughout the time period—to never stop writing. It doesn't matter what they write (see example above) as long as they keep the pen moving!
	▶ Encourage participants to write without outlining or planning their writing first.
	▶ Instruct participants not to correct or edit their writing at all.
	▶ Determine ahead of time whether you'll allow spontaneous discussion while people are writing. Some may find it distracting (or even rude), while others may appreciate the audio stimulation.
Try these variations . . .	▶ Have participants do this on a laptop rather than with pen and paper. Encourage them to never have more than 2 seconds without the click of a key!
	▶ Use the variation above, but tell them to turn off their monitors. This will help them to not correct errors or go back and read what they wrote right away.
	▶ Give this assignment as homework before a brainstorming session. Every day for a week, spend 5 minutes just writing about the topic to be discussed. Participants bring their writings to the session, and can refer to them for inspiration during the brainstorming.
	▶ Rather than write, have participants pair up. On your signal, Participant A of the pair will respond to your Focus Question and speak to Participant B nonstop for 4 minutes (following the guidelines above for writing). Switch roles and repeat. Then begin the selected brainstorming technique from Chapter 4, asking participants to draw their ideas from what they said as well as what they heard from their partner.

JEOPARDY

This is . . . ► A creativity exercise where participants must respond according to specific speech patterns.

What it does . . . ► Forces participants' brains to operate differently (and thus encourages creativity) as they must speak their responses in a different format than usual.
► Encourages and builds upon initial individual input as participants hear others' responses worded differently.

One drawback is . . . ► Some participants may find it frustrating to have to pause and reword their great responses.

What you need . . . ► No additional material.

Here's how . . .
1. Select and prepare to use a brainstorming technique from Chapter 4.
2. Review the purpose of the session with the group.
3. Review and get agreement on the four rules of brainstorming (see Chapter 1).
4. Turn the Focus Question you've developed into a statement.
5. Explain that all responses must be offered in the form of a question or they will not be recorded. You may want to stress the name of this activity (you don't ordinarily) because it will help the participants "get it."
6. State the "Focus Statement" and start the clock.
7. Brainstorm, using the technique you selected.

8. Sort or prioritize using the methods in Chapter 6 or 7.

For example . . .
► If the goal is to identify ways to shorten the time it takes to get expenses reimbursed, the Focus Statement may be, "This is one of the ways we will speed up the expense reimbursements." Antoine may think: manager approval limits should be higher. He would then use the format from TV's game show *Jeopardy* by saying, "What is 'increase manager approval limits'?" Just forcing himself to respond in the form of a question may inspire him (or those who hear the question) to think differently going forward.

Tips for success . . .
► Depending on the brainstorming technique used, this exercise can work with any group size.
► If you don't adhere to the question format requirement, the session will quickly revert to a more traditional brainstorming session—not necessarily a bad thing, but you will lose the creative feature of this exercise.
► Rather than record the entire question, capture the essence followed by a question mark.

Try these variations . . .
► Require that each response be sung to a common tune, or a made-up tune.
► If the group is multilingual, have them respond in only their non-native language.
► Conduct the session in "pig Latin." This is a form of language derived from ordinary English often used by children. Move the first consonant or consonant cluster of each word to the end of the word and add a long "a" sound, as in *eak-spay ig-pay atin-Lay* for *speak pig Latin.*
► Require that each response be given in one- or two-syllable words; that it be said in 10 words or less; or that it follow some other rule that causes participants to word their responses differently than they typically would do.

LET'S GET PHYSICAL

This is . . .
- A creativity exercise where participants change their physical position or location to inspire new and different ideas.

What it does . . .
- Raises the energy in the room.
- Engages the participants physically.
- Shifts participants' physical and visual perspective within the room.

One drawback is . . .
- Participants with certain physical disabilities or limitations may find this difficult.

What you need . . .
- No additional material.

Here's how . . .
1. Select and prepare to use a brainstorming technique from Chapter 4.
2. Review the purpose of the session with the group.
3. Review and get agreement on the four rules of brainstorming (see Chapter 1).
4. Have all the participants stand up.
5. Ask the Focus Question and start the clock.
6. Brainstorm, using the technique you selected.
7. Participants remain standing until the brainstorming session time is up.
8. Sort or prioritize using the methods in Chapter 6 or 7.

Tips for success . . .	➤ This exercise can work with any group size. ➤ If using one of the variations below, be conscious about the physical layout of the room. Remove anything that may compromise the safety of the group.
Try these variations . . .	➤ Conduct the brainstorming session while all participants are seated on large pillows on the floor; on their knees; straddling their chairs; sitting on a table; or in some other slightly uncomfortable position. The point is to change their physical body position. ➤ Have participants sit. They stand when they have a response. Remain standing until it is recorded. This activity not only raises the energy in the room, but also ensures ideas are not missed. ➤ Reverse the variation above: participants sit when they have a response. They remain seated until their response is recorded, then they stand back up. ➤ Conduct the brainstorming session while participants constantly wander around the room. They stop only to offer a response. After their response is recorded, they resume wandering. ➤ Take a field trip. Conduct the brainstorming session in a park, at a restaurant, in an elevator, in the cafeteria, in the boiler room, etc.

MIND READER

This is . . .
➤ A creativity exercise where participants try to antici-pate what their colleagues will say.

What it does . . .
➤ Gets participants into a different mindset that will inspire different perspectives.
➤ Encourages and builds upon initial individual input.
➤ Helps draw out shy or reluctant participants.

One draw-back is . . .
➤ This activity slows down the brainstorming as it takes more time to write than to speak.

What you need . . .
➤ The name of each participant on a different piece of paper.
➤ A pen for each participant.

Here's how . . .
1. Review the purpose of the session with the group.
2. Review and get agreement on the four rules of brain-storming (see Chapter 1).
3. Distribute the papers (making sure no one gets their own name).
4. Explain that when you start the clock, participants are to write down their own responses as well as the responses they anticipate or guess would be given by the person whose name is on their paper. They will have 3 minutes.
5. Ask the Focus Question and start the clock.
6. Participants record both kinds of responses.
7. When the clock stops, have the participants share all their responses while you record them. They do not need to tell you whose name was on their paper, nor

do they need to say which ideas were their own and which were "channeled."

8. Ask the Focus Question again and have the group build on the ideas previously given.
9. Sort or prioritize using the methods in Chapter 6 or 7.

Tips for success . . .
- This activity works best with smaller groups of participants who know each other well.
- Remind the group that there is no right or wrong answer. The point is not to be accurate in guessing what others might say, but to use that approach to get out more creative ideas. Discourage comments like "Oh, I would never have said that!"
- Don't ask the participants to state whether the idea they gave was from their perspective or the perspective of the other person—that's not important. What's important is the idea itself, regardless of where it came from!
- Save time by not recording duplicate responses.

Try these variations . . .
- Have a second round. Swap names. Now write what ideas *that* person would give based on all the ideas that are already posted.
- Skip the paper. Participants respond how anyone but themselves may respond to the Focus Question.
- Post one flip chart page per participant, with a different participant's name at the top of each. Give all participants a marker. After being asked the Focus Question, participants circulate the room and record on a participant's chart how they think that person might respond.
- If a member of the group cannot attend the session, have everyone who is there answer on behalf of the absent one—anticipating how he or she might have contributed.
- Combine this method with one of the brainstorming techniques in Chapter 4.

OBJECTS

This is . . .
- A creativity exercise where participants gain inspiration by associating random things with the topic.

What it does . . .
- Calls on one of our senses—touch—to help generate ideas.
- Adds interesting fun (through objects) to the brainstorming.
- Encourages cross-pollination of ideas as the group shares the objects.

One drawback is . . .
- Some participants may get distracted by the many objects provided.

What you need . . .
- A supply of unrelated objects. Include as many different textures as you can.

Here's how . . .
1. Select and prepare to use a brainstorming technique from Chapter 4.
2. Review the purpose of the session with the group.
3. Review and get agreement on the four rules of brainstorming (see Chapter 1).
4. Distribute the objects to the participants.
5. Explain that their challenge is to associate their object to the Focus Question.
6. Ask the Focus Question and start the clock.
7. Brainstorm, using the technique you selected.
8. Sort or prioritize using the methods in Chapter 6 or 7.

For example . . .	➤ Objects can be anything: a hairbrush, a can of corn, a twig, a paper clip, a child's toy, a golf tee, a bottle cap, a DVD, a straw, a calculator, a stuffed animal, a clump of pencil shavings, a hammer, and so on.
Tips for success . . .	➤ Depending on the brainstorming technique used, this exercise can work with any group size.
	➤ Be sure the participants handle, feel, or hold the items. Part of the creative inspiration comes from the sense of touch and feel.
	➤ The more varied the objects, the better.
Try these variations . . .	➤ Use the sense of smell to force associations. Rather than objects, bring things that have distinct odors and encourage the participants to smell them before responding. Items may include jars of spices (cinnamon, sage, rosemary, basil, vanilla, etc.), a peach, a chocolate bar, a flower, cologne, and so on.
	➤ Use *only* the sense of touch. Put each item in a box or bag. Participants may touch, but not look at the object. Use things with a unique texture such as a Koosh® ball, a block, a piece of sand paper, an inflated balloon, a cotton ball, an ice cube, a bunch of rubber bands, a pile of yarn or string, a wad of clay, and so on.
	➤ Have the participants bring random objects and then swap them in place of step 4 above.

PICTURES

This is . . .
- A creativity exercise where participants gain brainstorming inspiration by looking at many different pictures in magazines.

What it does . . .
- Calls on one of our senses—vision—to help generate ideas.
- Adds visual interest to the brainstorming.
- Encourages cross-pollination of ideas as the group shares the images.

One drawback is . . .
- Some participants may get distracted by the many, many pictures (and even the articles) in the magazines.

What you need . . .
- Several magazines per participant—the more varied the magazines, and the more pictures in them, the better.

Here's how . . .
1. Select and prepare to use a brainstorming technique from Chapter 4.
2. Review the purpose of the session with the group.
3. Review and get agreement on the four rules of brainstorming (see Chapter 1).
4. Distribute the magazines to the group. Be sure participants have access to many (if not all) of the magazines at once.
5. Tell the group to flip through the magazines and use the visual images to spark ideas for input.
6. Ask the Focus Question and start the clock.
7. Brainstorm, using the technique you selected.

8. Sort or prioritize using the methods in Chapter 6 or 7.

<table>
<tr><td>Tips for success . . .</td><td>

➤ This activity can work for any size group.

➤ Tell them to bring their reading glasses to the session.

➤ The more magazines, the better. The more varied the magazines, the better. The more pictures, the better.

➤ Encourage the participants to flip through the magazines quickly. Don't let them dwell on any page too long or they may start reading. Make a 5-second rule—the page must be turned within 5 seconds of seeing it.

➤ Don't let them interpret or even describe the picture, just give their idea. It doesn't matter how the picture helped them get to the idea, especially since it may not have even done so!

</td></tr>
</table>

Tips for success . . .

➤ This activity can work for any size group.

➤ Tell them to bring their reading glasses to the session.

➤ The more magazines, the better. The more varied the magazines, the better. The more pictures, the better.

➤ Encourage the participants to flip through the magazines quickly. Don't let them dwell on any page too long or they may start reading. Make a 5-second rule—the page must be turned within 5 seconds of seeing it.

➤ Don't let them interpret or even describe the picture, just give their idea. It doesn't matter how the picture helped them get to the idea, especially since it may not have even done so!

Try these variations . . .

➤ Cut various pictures from magazines (or print them from the Internet) and place them so all participants can easily shuffle through them. This helps prevent the group from getting distracted by the articles in the magazines.

➤ Post many pictures on the walls around the room (the more the better). Participants wander about the room, looking at the pictures and giving answers to the Focus Question.

➤ For process improvement sessions, have participants look for a picture that represents the current state of the process, and the future states with and/or without action, then share with the rest of the group.

➤ Ask the participants to be the ones to each bring many magazines or many pictures from magazines or the Internet.

➤ Before starting the brainstorming session, have the participants leaf through the magazines and just cut/rip out pictures for use later. Then follow the steps above using the pictures cut out by the participants.

► Download hundreds of very random images from the Internet and display/project them to the group in rapid succession (2–5 seconds per image). If you can't set the images to change automatically, appoint a participant to change the images so you are free to record the group's input.

REVERSE BRAINSTORMING

This is . . .
- A creativity exercise where participants brainstorm for the opposite of what they really want or need.

What it does . . .
- Reverses the thinking for participants, encouraging different perspectives.
- Allows participants to explore and even have fun with their cynical sides.
- Promotes creativity around topics that participants may be tired of brainstorming about (ways to improve customer service, ways to cut costs, etc.).

One drawback is . . .
- This activity may cause participants to become too cynical or discouraged about finding viable solutions.

What you need . . .
- No additional material.

Here's how . . .
1. Select and prepare to use a brainstorming technique from Chapter 4.
2. Create your Focus Question.
3. Use that Focus Question to create a new one that is exactly opposite.
4. Review the purpose of the session with the group.
5. Review and get agreement on the four rules of brainstorming (see Chapter 1).
6. Ask Opposite Focus Question you created beforehand and start the clock.
7. Brainstorm, using the technique you selected.
8. Revisit each item recorded and reverse it to make it applicable to the original Focus Question.

9. Sort or prioritize using the methods in Chapter 6 or 7.

For example . . .
- The Original Focus Question might have been, "Think about what it's like to be a customer who's been disappointed. You expect the organization to do something to rectify the problem, but also something to somehow make it up to you, right? You want them to help you so that you will come back again and again. So, what things need to be done to ensure customers feel well treated when they have a complaint?" Reversing this would create your Opposite Focus Question. "Think of how annoying customer complaints can be. They come as interruptions to your other work. They believe that we'll somehow resolve problems for them quickly and fairly. And all because they erroneously think we want them to come back to bother us again! So, let's start a list, how could we drive these customers away for good?"
- At step 8, a response like "let all phone calls go to voicemail" would be reversed to "don't allow any phone calls to go to voicemail" or "make sure all phone calls are answered by the second ring."

Tips for success . . .
- Depending on the brainstorming technique used, this exercise can work with any group size.
- During Step 8 above, draw out more than one response from each original one given to the Opposite Focus Question (see example above).

Try these variations . . .
- Add even more fun (and silliness) by awarding a prize to the "best response" to the Opposite Focus Question. In the example above, it would be to whoever finds the best way to get rid of your customers!
- Rather than creating an Opposite Focus Question, create one that purposefully goes after mediocrity. For example, "What's the bare minimum we can do to just avoid getting in trouble for the way we handle a complaining customer?"

ROLES

This is . . .

► A creativity exercise where participants consider the topic from different people's perspectives.

What it does . . .

► Gets participants into a different mindset that will inspire different perspectives.

► Adds an element of fun as participants may go so far as to take on the role of the name they are given.

One drawback is . . .

► The different roles and possible role playing may be distracting for some, or seem silly.

What you need . . .

► At least one slip of paper per participant—each slip has a different name printed on it.

Here's how . . .

1. Select and prepare to use a brainstorming technique from Chapter 4.
2. Review the purpose of the session with the group.
3. Review and get agreement on the four rules of brainstorming (see Chapter 1).
4. Distribute the slips of paper.
5. Encourage participants to consider the Focus Question from the perspective of the person whose name they are holding, and respond accordingly.
6. Ask the Focus Question and start the clock.
7. Brainstorm, using the technique you selected.
8. Sort or prioritize using the methods in Chapter 6 or 7.

| For example . . . | ▶ Names to use may include: Abraham Lincoln, Lady Gaga, Bugs Bunny, Rosa Parks, a six-year old schoolgirl, Spiderman, Marie Antoinette, an alien, Buddha, an Olympics silver medalist, an Apache warrior, Santa Claus, Sonia Sotomayor, a puppy, Harry Potter, and Muhammad Ali. |

Tips for success . . .
- ▶ This exercise works well with any size group and in combination with any brainstorming technique.
- ▶ Use names from many different sources: historical, fictional, classes of people (a six-year old schoolgirl, an Olympics silver medalist, an old man on his deathbed, etc.), celebrities, heroes and villains, professions, etc.
- ▶ Use controversial people to encourage truly different, creative thinking (Jack Kevorkian, Harvey Milk, Attila the Hun, Marie Antoinette, etc.)
- ▶ The goal is to promote creative thinking. If a role doesn't work for someone, don't force it.
- ▶ If someone can't use the name they drew, have a few extras available for them to substitute.

Try these variations . . .
- ▶ After a few moments, have participants swap roles.
- ▶ Do the brainstorming in several short rounds. For each round, have a new set of roles ready.
- ▶ Use the above variation. Each round has a group of roles that are related. Perhaps Round 1 is all cartoon characters; Round 2 is all historical figures, etc.
- ▶ Have blank slips of paper ready. Explain the exercise and have the participants choose whose perspective they would like to see considered. Write that name on the slip of paper and then swap papers and continue with step 5 above.
- ▶ Use only names or departments of key stakeholders. The CEO, the board, admin staff, marketing, customers, vendors, government agencies, competitors, unions, and so on.
- ▶ Begin any brainstorming technique. Use this exercise after that technique has run its course and you still need more creativity.

- ▶ Assign the same role to the entire room at once. The whole group thinks like the Tin Man from the Wizard of Oz, then like Mother Theresa, then like a high school valedictorian.
- ▶ Add an element of mystery by asking the participants to not disclose what role they have until after the brainstorming is over. Later, see if participants can guess who was being who.

SIX PERSPECTIVES

This is . . .   ➤ A creativity exercise where participants brainstorm in rounds, considering the topic from six different perspectives.

What it does . . .   ➤ Gets participants into a different mindset that will create different perspectives.
                          ➤ Liberates participants to be cynical and judging as well as optimistic and creative.

One drawback is . . .   ➤ Some participants may get frustrated when others offer responses that are not in sync with the perspective being explored at the moment.

What you need . . .   ➤ No additional material

Here's how . . .
1. Select and prepare to use a brainstorming technique from Chapter 4.
2. Review the purpose of the session with the group.
3. Review and get agreement on the four rules of brainstorming (see Chapter 1).
4. Explain that you will conduct the brainstorming in six short rounds.
5. During the first round, all participants should respond to the Focus Question from an analytical perspective.
6. Tell them there will be 2- to 3-minute time limits for each round.
7. Ask the Focus Question and start the clock.

8. Brainstorm, using the technique you selected.

9. Start a second round of brainstorming, using a different perspective. Then a third, etc.

10. Sort or prioritize using the methods in Chapter 6 or 7.

For example . . .
- ➤ Round 1: analytical/critical
- ➤ Round 2: ethical/moral
- ➤ Round 3: optimistic/opportunistic
- ➤ Round 4: pessimistic/devil's advocate
- ➤ Round 5: people/social
- ➤ Round 6: intuition/hunches

Tips for success . . .
- ➤ Depending on the brainstorming technique used, this exercise can work with any group size.
- ➤ Remember, there is no right or wrong answer in brainstorming. As participants start to respond in a particular round, someone may want to critique a response that "should" be given in a different round. Don't allow it. Remind them that the rounds are not to control the answers, but to *promote* answers—it doesn't matter when or how the great ideas come up, just that they do!
- ➤ Post the perspective title as you use it so participants remember which one to reference.

Try these variations . . .
- ➤ Divide the group into six teams. Assign a different perspective to each group and have them brainstorm in their teams using their perspective. Share results with the entire group and then sort and prioritize using an activity from Chapter 6 or 7.
- ➤ Use the variation above. Have teams swap perspectives one or more times before sharing results with the large group.
- ➤ Write the six perspectives on slips of paper and distribute to the group. If you have more than six participants, there will be duplicates. Conduct the brainstorming session while participants use their perspective to promote creative responses.

➤ Write the six perspectives on six flip charts and post them around the room (see Figure 5–2). Have the participants wander about the room, writing their responses on the charts as they feel them.

➤ Replace the suggested perspectives with others that are relevant to your organization: finance, human resources, marketing, legal, operations, etc.

FIGURE 5-2

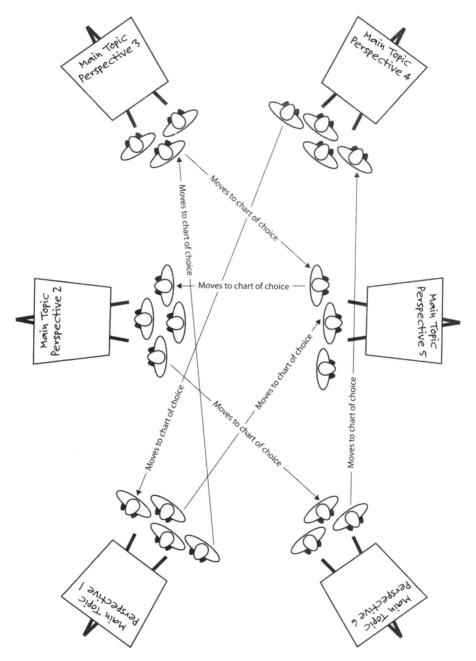

STOP AND START

This is . . .

- A creativity exercise where participants brainstorm in short bursts, mixed with periods of silence.

What it does . . .

- Prompts creativity by alternating between high energy brainstorming input and low energy quiet time.
- Gives participants a chance to internally process others' responses so they can build on them.
- Encourages and builds upon initial individual input.

Drawbacks are . . .

- This activity may bring down the energy level in the room during the silent period.
- Impatient participants may find the silent periods extremely frustrating.

What you need . . .

- One board (flip chart, white board, etc.) and a marker.
- A stopwatch or timer.

Here's how . . .

1. Review the purpose of the session with the group.
2. Review and get agreement on the four rules of brainstorming (see Chapter 1).
3. Ask the Focus Question and start the clock for 4 minutes.
4. When time is up, start the clock for 3 minutes of complete and total silence. During this time, participants reflect on what was already said as well as what else they'd like to add.
5. After 3 minutes, ask the Focus Question again and start the clock for 4 minutes.

6. Repeat Steps 5 and 6 as desired.

7. Sort or prioritize using the methods in Chapter 6 or 7.

Tips for success . . .
- This exercise can work with any group size.
- Be strict with quiet time. Enforce "complete and total silence" throughout the entire time period.

Try these variations . . .
- Divide the group into two teams. Have Team A brainstorm aloud while Team B experiences their quiet time for 4 minutes. Then switch so Team B brainstorms aloud while Team A has quiet time
- Distribute pen and paper. Allow participants to jot down notes during quiet time.
- Allow participants to contribute during quiet time by writing on the board. Use a board that is large enough to accommodate many participants at once. Or use sticky notes. Have several pads available, along with several markers. Participants record their response on the sticky note, then post it.

STORYTELLERS

This is . . .
➤ A creativity exercise where participants tell stories to each other about some random theme before brainstorming for creativity.

What it does . . .
➤ Creates memories and images for participants that will spark different, creative thinking.
➤ Creates warmth and closeness among the group.

One drawback is . . .
➤ This activity may be frustrating for impatient participants as they must wait until they are allowed to share their ideas.

What you need . . .
➤ No additional material.

Here's how . . .
1. Select and prepare to use a brainstorming technique from Chapter 4.
2. Review the purpose of the session with the group.
3. Review and get agreement on the four rules of brainstorming (see Chapter 1).
4. Prepare a story theme to be used (see examples below).
5. Explain that each participant will be invited to share a story about the topic given.
6. Start the clock for the first participant to tell his or her story in 60 (or 90) seconds.
7. After everyone has had a turn to tell their story, ask the Focus Question and start the clock.
8. Brainstorm, using the technique you selected.

9. Sort or prioritize using the methods in Chapter 6 or 7.

For example . . .

► Story themes should be simple things that everyone will have in common. Stories from childhood are often best. Tell stories about your favorite toy or activity growing up, your favorite birthday, a recent vacation, what dinner time was like when you were a kid, what you did during summer break, family traditions, and so on.

Tips for success . . .

► This exercise is best for smaller teams of less than 10 participants (more than that, and this will seem interminable!).

► Allow participants to pass if they have nothing to tell. The goal is not to hear the stories; it's to use the stories as inspiration for generating responses to the Focus Question.

► Encourage participants to be respectful (quiet!) while others share their stories.

► This is story time, not discussion time. Do not allow questions or dialogues.

► Choose a theme that is slightly related to the topic. If the topic is how to improve the hiring process, for example, perhaps the theme could be your very first job.

Try these variations . . .

► Have a board and marker ready. Allow participants to jump up and record their ideas as they have them (instead of waiting until everyone is finished). The storyteller should continue with his or her story while the participants are recording their ideas— don't stop or slow down.

► Rather than tell a story with words, act it out with charades or draw it on a board. Keep the time limit short. The goal is not to understand the story well, but to be inspired to have responses to the Focus Question.

WEB SURFING

This is . . . ➤ A creativity exercise where participants surf the Internet to get inspiration.

What it does . . . ➤ Appeals to participants who love technology.
➤ Stimulates ideas visually (with the images on websites) as well as verbally (with the words on websites).
➤ Allows participants joining the brainstorming session virtually to participate on equal footing.

One drawback is . . . ➤ Participants may get too distracted by the various interesting websites they come upon.

What you need . . . ➤ Laptop or computer with Internet access.
➤ Projector and screen.

Here's how . . . 1. Select and prepare to use a brainstorming technique from Chapter 4.
2. Review the purpose of the session with the group.
3. Review and get agreement on the four rules of brainstorming (see Chapter 1).
4. Find a search engine on the Internet and project it so all can see.
5. Ask three participants for a random word each. Put all three words in the search engine and search.
6. Ask another participant to choose any number. Click on the search result that corresponds to that number.
7. Scroll slowly down the site, encouraging participants

to use the images and/or words to prompt creative responses to the Focus Question.

8. Ask the Focus Question and start the clock.
9. Brainstorm, using the technique you selected.
10. Repeat steps 5 through 9 until time is over.
11. Sort or prioritize using the methods in Chapter 6 or 7.

Tips for success . . .

▶ Depending on the brainstorming technique used, this exercise can work with any group size.

▶ Keep this moving fast. Don't get tripped up navigating websites. Move quickly from site to site to site. Sometimes click on links within a site before going back to the search engine to find another random site, sometimes don't.

▶ Use an assistant. Your assistant can manage the website searches while you facilitate the brainstorming and record responses.

Try these variations . . .

▶ Have everyone use a laptop, smart phone, or other device that has Internet access. Give them random words (prepare a list ahead of time). Before they hit the search button, have them declare what numbered result they will click on from the search.

▶ Use the variation above, but have each participant use a different search engine.

▶ Use the first variation, but have participants work in pairs (this will prevent participants from getting distracted into just surfing the Web).

▶ Use the first variation, but when the search engine gives results, have them click "next page" repeatedly until you randomly tell them to stop. Then click on the first result of that page.

▶ Come prepared with slips of paper that have random words to use in place of step 5 above.

▶ Determine which search result to click on by rolling dice.

CHAPTER **6**

GROUPING METHODS

Use these activities to group or sort long lists of brainstormed ideas only. These methods will help you determine *how* to sort them. The resulting organization of data will aid in future analysis.

If the brainstorming activity has been lengthy, you might want to send the participants on a 10- to 20-minute break while you think about the sorting activity that may best suit the brainstorming results. (You may also want to clean up the room or rearrange the seating, to highlight that this is a different stage of the process.) Any materials called for in these grouping activities are, of course, in addition to what you've used in the brainstorming session itself.

Chapter 7 has activities for prioritizing brainstormed lists. Use those activities to evaluate, eliminate, rank, decide, or otherwise prioritize the raw brainstormed list, or to process the organized groupings that result from using the methods in this chapter.

ALPHABET CATEGORIES

This is . . .   ➤ A grouping method where participants sort the results from a brainstorming session into defined categories that they create.

What it does . . .   ➤ Helps maintain the neutrality of each category (none is perceived as being more important than another).
➤ Allows flexibility in creating, eliminating, or combining categories.

One drawback is . . .   ➤ Sometimes an early category may influence the entire sorting process—in a nonproductive way.

What you need . . .   ➤ One board (flip chart, white board, etc.) and a marker.

Here's how . . .   1. Review the purpose of the session with the group.
2. Review the results from the brainstorming session.
3. Make sure everyone understands each of the items being considered.
4. Have the group create a category name for one item on the list.
5. Record that category name on a separate chart, and label it A.
6. Place an A next to the matching item on the original list.
7. For the next item, ask if it fits in Category A.
8. If yes, place an A next to that item as well. If not, create a new category name, record it on the second chart under Category A, and label it B.

9. Place a B next to the matching item on the original list.

10. Repeat this process for all of the remaining items—each time asking if it fits in a category that has already been defined, or if it is the first in a new category.

For example . . .
▶ The group has brainstormed a list of possible company celebration activities. The first idea is a picnic. The group decides to call its category Outdoor Ideas. Label it A and put an A next to picnic. The next idea is a bingo night. They agree this is not an outdoor activity. So they create a new activity called Game Ideas. They label it B and place a B next to bingo night. The next idea is softball. They agree this is an outdoor activity and place an A next to it. Next is dinner out. They agree this doesn't fit any of the categories, so they create a new one called Relaxing Ideas and label it C, and so on. Figure 6–1 shows how this sorting process might work.

Tips for success . . .
▶ Use A, B, C, etc., rather than numbers 1, 2, 3, etc. Numbers suggest priority or emphasis and may detract from successful grouping. Colors can work, but only if the number of categories doesn't exceed the number of colored markers you have!

▶ Don't rush the naming of categories (see "drawback" above). Let the group toss a few ideas out before choosing.

▶ Be open to renaming categories—they may morph as they grow.

▶ If the number of categories is too great, combine them, but only after you've finished going through the entire list of items once. A general guideline is to aim for between three and ten categories.

Try these variations . . .
▶ Have the group look at the brainstormed list and suggest categories they'd like to use before addressing any single item. Record these category names and label them A, B, C, etc. As a group, decide which category is most appropriate for an item.

(text continues on page 124)

FIGURE 6-1

CATEGORIES

A Outdoors
B Games
C Relaxing
D Entertainment

► Use the variation above, but sort the list by filling categories first. Start with Category A and find all the items that belong in that category, labeling as you go. Then do the same for Category B, and so on.

CARD SORT

This is . . . ▶ A grouping method where participants sort a brain-stormed list into categories—permitting each item to be categorized in more than one place.

What it does . . . ▶ Avoids the inevitable conflict that arises when an item must be located into one and only one category.

▶ Frees up the group to sort items in a way that feels more accurate to them.

▶ Makes the activity physical as participants move cards about.

One draw-back is . . . ▶ Locating an item in too many categories may diminish the value of the categories altogether.

What you need . . . ▶ A packet of large (4" x 6" or even 5" x 8") index cards.

▶ A marker.

Here's how . . . 1. While the participants are on break, write the ideas from the brainstormed list onto the index cards—one idea per card. Often one or two of the participants will volunteer to help with this (accept with alacrity!).

2. Review the purpose of the session with the group.

3. Review the results from the brainstorming session.

4. Make sure everyone understands each of the options being considered.

5. Have the group create categories for sorting the cards.

6. Read each card aloud, and ask the participants to determine which category it belongs in. If a card fits more than one category, have a scribe create a duplicate card and place the cards in both categories. A six-category card sort is illustrated in Figure 6–2.

Tips for success . . .

➤ Try to limit the number of duplicate cards that are made. The more you have, the more you run the risk of diluting the usefulness of the categories. If this happens, revisit the categories—are they really helpful?

Try these variations . . .

➤ Rather than sorting card by card, sort by whole categories. Start with the first category and ask, "Which of the items belong in this category?" Be sure to have someone make duplicate cards of items already located in other categories.

➤ Distribute the cards randomly to individuals. Have them put them into categories; tell them to make duplicates if they feel a particular idea belongs in more than one category. Then, have the group review the categories together and make adjustments (and more duplicates, if necessary).

➤ Use the variation above, but do it in teams instead of individually.

FIGURE 6-2

LEADERLESS

This is . . .
- A grouping method where participants work together to organize the results of their brainstorming session without being directed or facilitated.

What it does . . .
- Raises the energy in the room as participants scramble to quickly organize the input.
- Allows for a free-flowing of opinions as the group resolves differences without intervention.
- Reinforces for the group that they own the results of the brainstorming session.

One drawback is . . .
- The sorting process may be dominated by one or two participants who overpower others.

What you need . . .
- One board (flip chart, white board, etc.) and a few markers.

Here's how . . .
1. Review the purpose of the session with the group.
2. Review the results from the brainstorming session.
3. Make sure everyone understands each of the options being considered.
4. Tell the group they have only 15 minutes to organize the brainstorming results; then the group will move into the next phase—analyzing, implementing, prioritizing, or whatever is the ultimate goal of the grouping activity.

Tips for	▶ This activity works best with groups of fewer than
success . . .	eight. With larger groups, a few participants will
	likely step forward and facilitate the process—and

**Tips for
success . . .**

▶ This activity works best with groups of fewer than eight. With larger groups, a few participants will likely step forward and facilitate the process—and may be perceived as trying to control or manipulate the process. For larger groups, use the team variation below.

▶ This activity works best with participants who have healthy, open, cooperative relationships with each other.

▶ Adjust the time limit to the needs of the group. The larger the group and/or the larger the list, the more time they will need.

**Try these
variations . . .**

▶ Divide the group into teams. Have the teams follow the steps above. Then have the teams share their groupings with each other and reconcile differences together.

▶ For smaller groups, use the above variation except have them do it individually.

QUICK SORT

This is . . .   ► A grouping method where participants quickly sort a list of brainstormed items according to a few basic, predetermined criteria.

What it does . . .   ► Makes the initial sorting of a brainstormed list quick and easy, which gives the group an almost immediate sense of accomplishment.
    ► Frames the grouping process with easy-to-understand criteria.
    ► Provides a stepping stone to other grouping or prioritization activities.

One draw-back is . . .   ► This way of grouping results may not be very precise.

What you need . . .   ► One board (flip chart, white board, etc.) and a marker.

Here's how . . .
1. Review the purpose of the session with the group.
2. Review the results from the brainstorming session.
3. Make sure everyone understands each of the options being considered.
4. Sort the brainstormed items into a few predetermined categories (see "Tips" below).
5. Move quickly through the list.
6. Set aside items for further consideration if there is not a quick consensus. Do not linger.
7. Go back and revisit items set aside during the first pass.

For example . . .	► Categories could be: high/medium/low cost; easy/ medium/difficult implementation; yes/no/maybe; high/medium/low feasibility; new/adapted/reuse of the current state; Department A, B, C, or D; and so on.
	► Binary choice categories could be: feasible/not feasible; requires higher authority/we can approve; significant/minimal impact; more research required/ not required; and so on.

Tips for success . . .	► Move quickly, but not so quickly that slower participants get ignored or left behind.
	► Determine the sorting criteria beforehand. You may do this before the meeting even starts, or wait until the brainstorming is over. Send the group on a break and use their brainstormed list to inspire your sorting criteria.
	► Most participants find two to four categories to be the most comfortable to work with.
	► Use this activity when it's not critical to get the items in a "right" category. Often this means that you plan to do something else to the sorted list before taking action.

Try these variations . . .	► Have the group determine the sorting categories once they look over the brainstormed list.
	► Write the ideas on index cards and sort them physically into the categories. This allows the group to move the ideas around a bit until they are comfortable that they've found a good fit for each one.
	► Use categories that are not mutually exclusive, for example cost, impact, and speed. Each idea will satisfy those criteria to some degree or another. The goal in the Quick Sort is to associate an idea with one of those three criteria that it matches best. For example, if the group is sorting ideas to improve their hiring process, the idea "outsource reference checks" has cost, impact, and speed implications. The group may determine that the speed benefit is

the most important element of this option, and put it in that category.

▸ An even quicker sort: categorize every item as "no" or "maybe." This will help the group quickly eliminate all the ideas that are not really feasible from those that are, or at least may be.

SYMBOLS

This is . . .   ➤ A grouping method where participants categorize brainstorming results first and *then* label those categories.

What it does . . .   ➤ Encourages participants to group options without being limited or influenced by category labels.
➤ Forces participants to stay focused on the options and groupings as they happen.

One drawback is . . .   ➤ This process may be frustrating or difficult for some participants who want a category label to help them categorize.

What you need . . .   ➤ Large (4" x 6" or even 5" x 8") index cards (one for each option, plus 20 or so extras).
➤ Tape.
➤ A marker.

Here's how . . .

1. Review the purpose of the session with the group.
2. Review the results from the brainstorming session.
3. Make sure everyone understands each of the options being considered.
4. Put each option on a separate index card and post them so everyone can see them.
5. Ask the group to identify two cards that "clearly" belong in the same category.
6. Repost those two cards together slightly away from the rest of the cards.

7. Create a label for this newly created category on another card, using an unrelated symbol, not a word. These symbols are not meant to represent the category, merely to distinguish it from other categories. See Figure 6–3 for an example of some symbols you might use.

8. Repeat steps 5 through 7 for another pairing that is separate and distinct from the first pairing.

9. Repeat this several more times, until there are no more obvious, easy pairings.

10. Next, ask the group to select one of the remaining cards that they feel belongs in a category already begun. When everyone agrees, repost that card into the category it fits.

11. Repeat step 10 until all the cards have been placed into one of the existing categories. Or, you may discover another new category that wasn't so obvious at step 5.

12. Have the group look at the contents of each category, and now define that category with word(s) to reflect the contents.

Tips for success . . .

► The fewer cards you have, the fewer new categories you'll create in step 8. Don't press to uncover all of the possible pairings. If you miss one, it will become apparent at step 11.

► Do not use symbols that relate to the category, or you defeat the primary benefit of this activity: participants categorizing things together *without* being limited or influenced by labels. The category may morph as more cards are added to it.

Try these variations . . .

► Divide into teams. Ask them to each do step 5 concurrently. After a few minutes, have them present their pairing to the group for group agreement. Continue from step 6 with the whole group, building off the pairings that the teams started.

(text continues on page 136)

FIGURE 6-3

 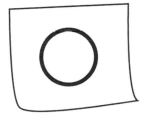 

➤ Post three or four category symbol cards away from the pool of option cards. Have participants do step 5 individually. Each participant will choose a pairing and post it under a symbol card. Have the group review and agree or adjust as necessary. Then proceed with the next steps together.

CHAPTER 7

PRIORITIZATION PROCESSES

Use these activities to evaluate, eliminate, rank, decide, or otherwise prioritize ideas generated in a brainstorming session. You may have used an activity from Chapter 6 to sort or group the ideas (if you haven't, you may want to do so before you go further); now you can use the activities in this chapter to prioritize or choose. Time limits given here are just suggestions. Adjust them to fit your topic, your group, and your situation. Err on the side of too long and adjust as necessary. It's better to give too much time for full analysis than not enough.

BALLOONS

This is . . .
- A prioritization process where participants use balloons to eliminate all but the very top option(s) generated in a brainstorming session.

What it does . . .
- Adds some fun through the use of balloons.
- Forces the group to make final decisions (that would be difficult to be revisited).
- Encourages the participants to consider each option one at a time.

One drawback is . . .
- This activity may seem too silly for some groups.

What you need . . .
- One inflated balloon for each idea or piece of input.
- A marker that will write on the balloon.

Here's how . . .
- Beforehand, write each of the results from the brainstorming session on inflated balloons—one idea per balloon.
- Review the purpose of the session with the group.
- Review the results from the brainstorming session.
- Make sure everyone understands each of the options being considered.
- Determine with the group how many ideas from the brainstorming session need to be eliminated from consideration.
- Take any balloon and ask the group if they want to keep the idea written on it, or not. If not, pop the balloon and the idea is eliminated.

▶ Repeat this for each balloon, one at a time, until you have the desired number of ideas (balloons) left.

Tips for success . . .

▶ This process can work for any size group.

▶ Practice writing on balloons beforehand so you get the knack of writing legibly on a soft, curved surface. Also check how long the ink remains wet on the balloon after writing so you can manage the drying time in the session.

▶ Blow the balloons up large enough that there is maximum surface space for writing, and also so they are easier to pop. Do this before the session begins.

▶ Bring extra balloons to allow for accidental breakage.

Try these variations . . .

▶ For larger groups, split into smaller teams. Give a portion of the balloons to each team and have them each create a set of balloons. Have them follow the above steps to eliminate the more obvious options. Each team will pop all of their balloons except for the top two or three (you decide!). Bring the entire group back together and follow steps 6 and 7 for the remaining balloons.

▶ Use helium to inflate the balloons. Tie a string to each one. As the group considers a balloon they are unsure of, release it back up to the ceiling for later reconsideration.

DOTS

This is . . . ▸ A prioritization process where participants use adhesive dots to vote for preferred alternatives from a brainstorming session.

What it does . . .
▸ Engages the participants physically.
▸ Allows all participants to readily see where support for options lie.
▸ Offers great versatility and flexibility.

One draw-back is . . .
▸ Participants' votes may be influenced as they see how others vote.

What you need . . .
▸ One adhesive circle label ("dot") for each participant.

Here's how . . .
1. Review the purpose of the session with the group.
2. Review the results from the brainstorming session.
3. Make sure everyone understands each of the options being considered.
4. Distribute the dots.
5. Participants will stick their dot next to the option they prefer. See Figure 7–1 for an example of what this might look like.
6. Count the dots. The option with the most dots wins.

Tips for success . . .
▸ Use dots that are at least ¾" in diameter (otherwise they are difficult to see from a distance).
▸ Encourage participants to vote in silence. If they speak, they may sway others as they are voting.

FIGURE 7-1

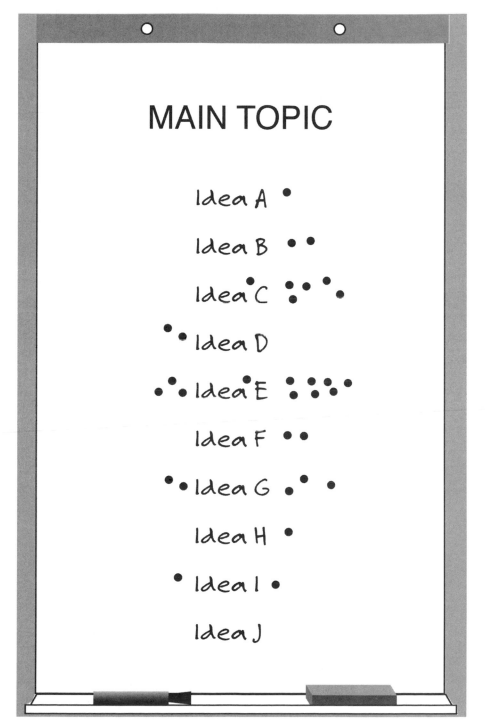

- Give participants a moment before asking them to vote. Let them consider the options and make their decisions before they get up. If you don't, they are more likely to follow the lead of the quicker or more vocal voters.
- Ties can easily be broken with a second round of voting.
- If there are more options than there are participants, use one of the variations below so you ensure at least one option will get more than one dot!

Try these variations . . .

- Give each participant more than one dot. Declare up front if they must use each dot for a different option, or if they can use two or more dots (votes) for a single option. The latter option allows them to give weight to their preferences.
- Use the variation above. Participants take turns putting up each dot. You may even allow them to make a plug for the option they just voted for. Use this variation when you want participants to influence each other as they vote.
- Use different-colored dots to carry different weight. For example: red counts as one vote; green counts as two votes; blue counts as four votes. Give each participant one dot of each color, and proceed as you did in the main activity.
- Use different-colored dots to indicate general ranking rather than a weighted vote. For example, red is a first choice; blue is a second choice; yellow is a third choice; and so on. After the voting, look for patterns or clusters of dots that will help the group draw its conclusions and make choices. Perhaps most of the blue dots are on the same option, or all of the yellow dots are on options that don't require extra financing.
- Use different-colored dots to indicate general preference. For example, yellow means high preference; green means medium preference; blue means low preference. You can give more than one of each color to each participant. As in the variation above, look

for patterns or clusters of dots that will help the group draw its conclusions and make choices.

➤ When you are trying to cut a large list down to something more manageable, a good guideline is to aim at eliminating all but 20 or 25 percent of the items. To do this, give each participant only as many dots as you want options to remain. For example, if you have 40 options and want to winnow down to 25 percent, give each participant 10 dots. After the voting, eliminate the 30 options that received the fewest votes.

➤ Sometimes participants are influenced by how others vote. Before voting, number each of the options. Tell the participants to write the number of their preferred option on their dot. Then when they stand up to vote, they will have to place the dot where they originally intended it, rather than be swayed by other voters.

➤ Make this process more confidential by turning the board or otherwise hiding the options. Participants vote one at a time in privacy so no one sees their votes. While this offers some confidentiality, participants who vote later may be more apt to be influenced by where they see dots when they vote. Consider using this in combination with the variation above. Or, have participants vote one dot at a time, so a single participant's voting early in the process doesn't overly influence others.

GRID-BASED DECISION

This is . . .
- A prioritization process where participants compare all options against each other in a grid.

What it does . . .
- Makes the group's decision-making process orderly and visible as they do it.
- Provides a disciplined approach to compare any conceivable combination of options.

One drawback is . . .
- This activity may seem tedious for some participants who see an obvious "winner" quickly.

What you need . . .
- Large writing surface (several flip chart pages posted; large white board; long piece of butcher paper).
- A marker.

Here's how . . .
1. Draw a large grid. List all the options at the head of each column, and in the same order, at the head of each row. (If this is a new session, or you've sent participants on a break, have this done when they enter the room.)
2. Label each option A, B, C, and so on.
3. Review the purpose of the session with the group.
4. Review the results from the brainstorming session.
5. Make sure everyone understands each of the options being considered.
6. Compare the option on the first row (Option A), with the option in the second column (Option B).
7. Indicate the group's preference by an A or B in the intersection of the row and column.

8. Working across, compare Option A to the rest of the options in the columns. For each pair, write the preference in the intersecting box.

9. Repeat this process for each row. Figure 7–2 illustrates what this might look like.

Tips for success . . .

▶ This activity works best when there are fewer options (because they will fit on the grid!).

▶ You will notice a diagonal appear across the grid where the options intersect with themselves. The lower left half of the grid is actually a mirror image of the upper right half. You only need to work the upper right half—don't repeat your efforts by completing the lower left half.

Try these variations . . .

▶ Divide the group into two teams. Have one team do the upper right half of the grid; the other team will do the lower left half. They can work quietly at opposite ends of the room, then go up and mark the chart. Compare results and reconcile differences.

▶ If you use this activity often, add variety by working down the columns instead of across the rows.

FIGURE 7-2

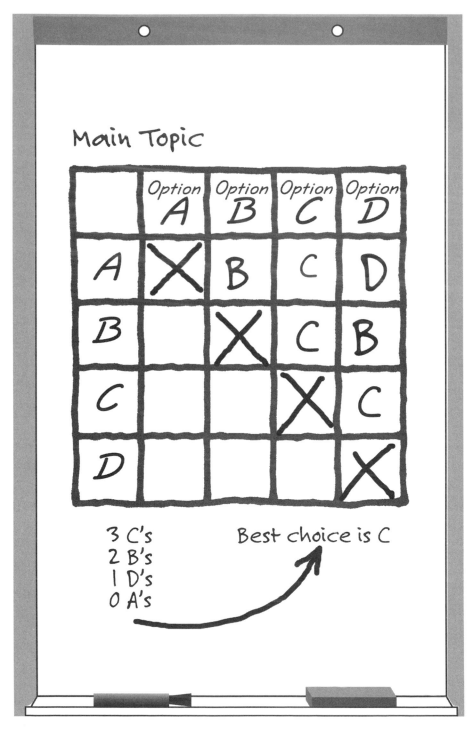

INVESTING IN IDEAS

This is . . .   ▸ A prioritization process where participants use play money to vote for their preferred idea(s) from a brainstorming session.

What it does . . .
▸ Adds some fun through the use of play money.
▸ Allows participants to vote for more than one option.
▸ Allows participants to indicate the relative strengths of their preferences for the options.

One drawback is . . .
▸ Using play money to represent preferences may seem a little gimmicky to some participants.

What you need . . .
▸ Play money in small denominations—enough for each participant to have $100 in twenties, tens, and fives.
▸ Tape (optional).

Here's how . . .
1. Review the purpose of the session with the group.
2. Review the results from the brainstorming session.
3. Make sure everyone understands each of the options being considered.
4. Distribute $100 play money to each participant.
5. Explain that they are to use their play money to "invest" in their favorite options.
6. Have them tape or otherwise affix their money to their preferred option.
7. They can "invest" as much or as little play money in as many or few options as they like.

8. The winning option is the one with the most money "invested."

For example . . .

- Lynn "invests" all $100 in Option B because she very, very strongly favors that option.
- Charlene "invests" $30 in Option B, $40 in Option C, and $30 in Option K because she likes all three of these about the same.
- William "invests" $50 in Option A, $10 in Option C, and $40 in Option L because he strongly favors Options A and L, but also has mild preference for Option C.

Tips for success . . .

- This process can work for any size group, but works better for groups fewer than 16 or so.

Try these variations . . .

- Make one of the denominations $50 so participants have to award half their vote to one option. Perhaps give them the option of trading the $50 bill to others to get smaller denominations from them.
- Give each participant fifty $1 bills instead of larger bills. This requires participants to differentiate more precisely.
- Do the activity in two or more rounds. After each round, select the options that received the most "investment." Give participants another set of $100 and repeat the activity for just the top choices from the prior round.
- Simplify the process by only using five $20 play money bills.
- Simplify the math for participants by only using ten $1 play money bills.

RANKED PAIRS

This is . . .
- A prioritization process where participants rank the results of a brainstorming session by looking at the results in pairs.

What it does . . .
- Makes the group's decision-making process visible as they do it.
- Helps the group rank their options from strongest to weakest.

One draw-back is . . .
- This activity may seem tedious for those participants who see an obvious order quickly.

What you need . . .
- Large (4" x 6" or even 5" x 8") index cards (one for each option).
- A marker.

Here's how . . .
- Review the purpose of the session with the group.
- Review the results from the brainstorming session.
- Make sure everyone understands each of the options being considered.
- Put each option on a separate index card.
- Arrange the index cards in any order in a line.
- Read aloud the first two options and ask the group to select the better one.
- Place that one in first place.
- Now compare the option that came in second to the third option and select the better one.
- Place the preferred option from that pairing in second place. Next compare the loser to the fourth option, and so on down the line.

| | ► | Begin again and go down the line of cards repeatedly until you make it through the line without making any changes. |

For example . . . ► The group has four options that they would prioritize. Each is written down on a different-colored card: green, blue, yellow, and pink. They begin to compare them, randomly. They compare green to blue and select blue. Blue goes into first place. They compare green to yellow and select green. It stays in second place. They compare yellow to pink and select pink. They move pink to third place. This is the line-up at the end of Round 1: blue, green, pink, yellow. In Round 2, they begin again by comparing blue to green. They again select blue, so it remains in first place. They compare green to pink and select pink. They move pink into second place. They compare green to yellow and select green, so it remains in third place. This is the line-up at the end of Round 2: blue, pink, green, yellow. Now for Round 3. They compare blue to pink and select pink. They move it into first place and then compare blue to green. They select blue, leave it where it is, and do the same for green and yellow. The end of Round 3: pink, blue, green, yellow. They go through the line of options one more time. When they select pink over blue, blue over green, and green over yellow, nothing moved and they know this is their final, ranked list. Look at Figure 7–3 to see how this might work.

Tips for success . . . ► Large index cards (4" x 6" or even 5" x 8") work best so participants can easily see them.

► Be careful not to rush the process. It can be tedious, but be vigilant about checking with all the participants before moving on.

Try these variations . . . ► As in the example above, sometimes very strong options begin at the end of the line. Once the group notices this, take these strong options and put them in first place before beginning Round 2. They will

FIGURE 7-3

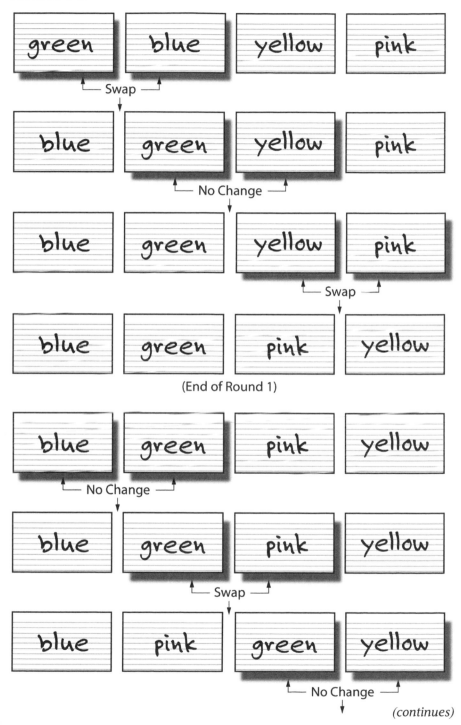

(End of Round 1)

(continues)

FIGURE 7-3 *(continued)*

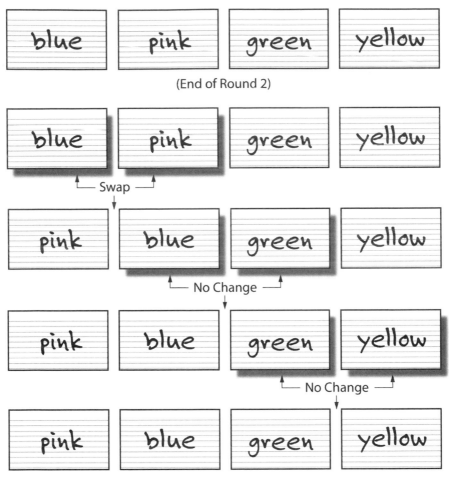

(End of Round 2)

Swap

No Change

No Change

(End of Round 3 and Final Ranking)

either stay there, or move down slightly as you continue, but you avoid doing round after round just to get them up in the order.

➤ Save time by replacing the random order in step 5 with someone making an initial ranking of the options (choose a member of the group at random). Then, as a group, go through the rest of the steps to adjust or fine-tune the order.

➤ Divide the group into teams and have each team do this process separately, then compare results.

PROS AND CONS

This is . . .
- A prioritization process where participants consider the pros and cons of their entire brainstormed list to select the best options.

What it does . . .
- Helps participants focus more on the risks and the benefits of each option, rather than fixating on a particular option.
- Gets participants into a different mindset that will promote different perspectives.

One draw-back is . . .
- It may be easy for participants to remember which card represents their preference, and use that to steer the discussion.

What you need . . .
- Index cards (two for each item on the brainstormed list; 4" x 6" or even 5" x 8") .
- A marker.

Here's how . . .
- Beforehand, write each option from the brainstormed list on two separate index cards.
- Review the purpose of the session with the group.
- Review the results from the brainstorming session.
- Make sure everyone understands each of the options being considered.
- As a group, quickly identify what the top three pros are for each option, and write them on the back of that card.
- Do the same for the cons of each option, writing them on the backs of the other set of cards.
- Shuffle the cards well.

- Spread the cards out face down, so only the pros and cons are showing, not the options themselves.
- Have the group discuss the pros and rank the cards from strongest to weakest; then do the same by cons.
- Turn over the cards to reveal the group's preferences.

Tips for success . . .
- This activity works best when the group has fewer options because of the time it takes to list the pros and cons for each option under consideration.
- Use different-colored index cards—one for the pros, one for the cons.

Try these variations . . .
- Use just one card per option. Write both pros and cons on the back of that card. This is a bit more efficient, but it may also make it easier for participants to identify which card is which option.
- After the cards have been ranked (step 9), discuss the patterns the group sees with the pros and/or cons. Use that discussion to drive agreement about decision criteria that should be used for selecting the best option. Then apply those criteria to another prioritization process in this chapter.

ROTATING CHARTS

This is . . .
- A prioritization process where small teams of participants assess the viability of alternatives from a brainstorming session.

What it does . . .
- Engages the participants with a fast pace and physical movement.
- Allows many participants (in teams) to review and prioritize information quickly and efficiently.

One drawback is . . .
- This activity prevents the whole group from hearing or participating in the richer discussions that only happened in the smaller teams.

What you need . . .
- One pad of large (4" x 6" or larger) stickies for each team.
- One marker for each team.
- As many flip charts (white boards, etc.) as there will be teams.

Here's how . . .
1. Beforehand, post the results from the brainstorming session in chunks, at stations around the room.
2. Review the purpose of the session with the group.
3. Review the results from the brainstorming session.
4. Make sure everyone understands each of the options being considered.
5. Divide the group into as many teams as there are stations.
6. Explain that teams will get 5 minutes to review and evaluate the input.

7. Teams put a check mark next to any item they feel is a viable option.
8. Teams put an "X" next to any item they feel is not at all viable.
9. Teams put a sticky next to any item they feel could be altered to become viable. On the sticky, they write how to improve it. For an example of what this activity might look like, see Figure 7–4.
10. Teams move to the next chart and repeat steps 6 through 9.
11. Repeat until the teams have been to all the stations.
12. As a group, consolidate the results and discuss for further analysis. Perhaps use another prioritization process to further pare down the list of options.

Tips for success . . .
▶ Use a different-colored pad of stickies for each team. This will help keep clear which team provided which feedback for later discussion or clarification.
▶ Team of between three and five participants work best.

Try these variations . . .
▶ For small groups, replace the teams with individual participants.
▶ Rather than using check marks, have teams rank the alternatives at each station. Tabulate the top options at each station and consolidate to find the top choice(s).

FIGURE 7-4

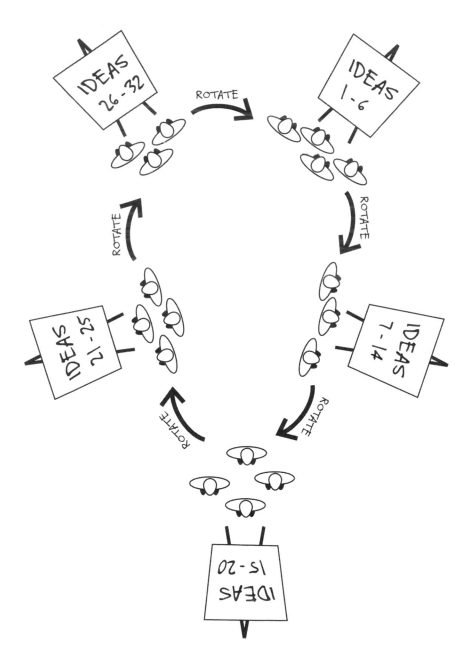

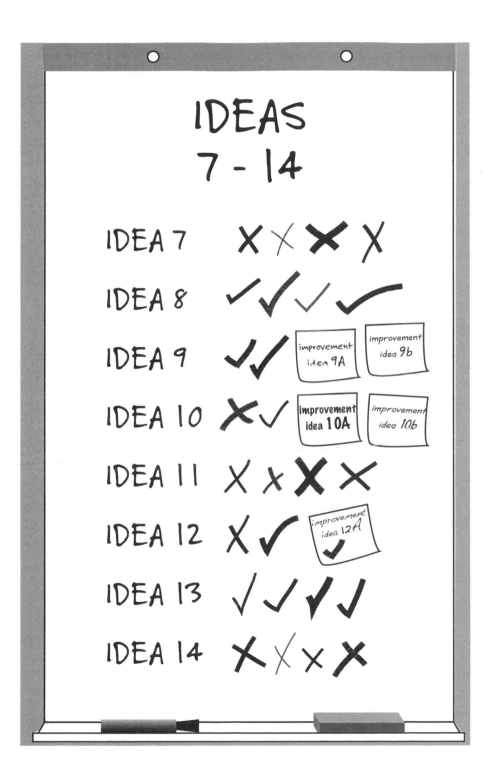

SEVEN

This is . . .
- A prioritization process where participants write their preferences on cards and swap them for individual ranking.

What it does . . .
- Raises the energy in the group because of the competition.
- Engages the participants with a fast pace and physical movement.
- Helps neutralize some of the more dominant members of the group.

One drawback is . . .
- This activity may encourage participants to vote in accordance with those who went before them.

What you need . . .
- One index card for each participant.
- A marker.
- A flip chart (white board, etc.).
- A stopwatch or timer.

Here's how . . .
1. You will need one option per participant, so before you begin, you may need to prioritize using an activity such as Dots (page 140) to winnow your brainstorming list.
2. Write one option per card.
3. Review the purpose of the session with the group.
4. Review the results from the brainstorming session.
5. Make sure everyone understands each of the options being considered.
6. Distribute one index card to each participant.

7. Have the participants stand together in a large, open area.
8. Start the clock for 15 seconds. Participants will swap their cards, face down, with each other. This should be done rapidly. Keep swapping over and over until time is called.
9. Start the clock for 1 minute. Participants quickly find a partner and together read their two cards.
10. They determine together how to distribute 7 points between the two cards, depending on how much they agree with each card.
11. Participants record their point allocations on the back of the card and prepare to swap again.
12. Have them repeat steps 6 through 9 for seven or more rounds (unless there are fewer than seven people in the group), always choosing a new partner. See Figure 7–5.
13. At the end of the activity, have participants tally the points of whatever card they end up with. On a flip chart, write down the number of points that each idea was awarded; the ideas with the highest scores are the top priorities for the group.

For example . . .

► The group is deciding among many ideas for a company celebration. After swapping, Patrick and Lin pair up. They have Cards A and B, and agree they favor Card A over Card B, but only slightly. They write 4 on the back of Card A and 3 on the back of Card B. After swapping, Patrick pairs with Donna, and they happen to get two cards neither has seen before. They both strongly prefer Card D over Card C. They write 6 on the back of Card D and 1 on the back of Card C. And so on.

Tips for success . . .

► This activity works well with larger groups, especially when there are many options and a clear group favorite is not apparent.
► Encourage participants to ignore the points already recorded on the backs of the cards when they evaluate them.

FIGURE 7-5

Round 1

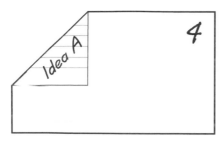

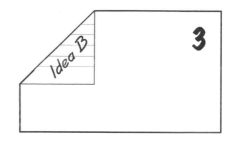

Round 2

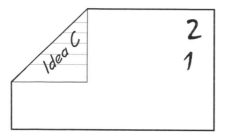

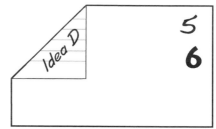

Round 3

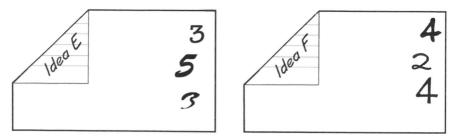

- ➤ Participants don't have to award any points to an option: it's okay to award 7 to one card and 0 to the other one.
- ➤ No fractions are permitted. As close as two options may be, the participant pairs must give one a slight edge by awarding only whole points.
- ➤ It's okay if a participant gets a card a second or even third time. They will be comparing against a different card, and with a different partner, so results will not be identical.

Try these variations . . .
- ➤ Rather than having the participants pair up, have them get into quick trios.
- ➤ Have the participants pair up and keep their partners for the rest of the activity. Swap all over the room, but when it's time to do steps 9 and 10, they bring the card they are holding back to each other and award points.
- ➤ Rather than just one item per card, write three. The comparison is then made between all three items on one card versus all three on the other card. Participants award points based on all three options on the card, not just one or two. This variation prompts discussion, sometimes violent discussion, as someone loves one of the ideas on a card, but two ideas on the other card and then has to choose—it causes stress (on purpose) and after the activity, some of that stress is vented and the group has a more-honest-than-otherwise-would-have-happened discussion about a few key ideas or a few pet ideas, etc. You might *not* want to use this variation with a group you have never worked with before.

SUDDEN DEATH

This is . . .
- A prioritization process where participants compare options to each other one at a time to find the single best one.

What it does . . .
- Forces the group to make absolute decisions that are not easily revisited.
- Helps the group to select one and only one final option.

One drawback is . . .
- This activity may cause the team to miss opportunities as they insist on reaching the one, final result.

What you need . . .
- One large (4" x 6" or even 5" x 8") index card for each option.
- A marker.

Here's how . . .
1. Beforehand, write each option on a separate card.
2. Review the purpose of the session with the group.
3. Review the results from the brainstorming session.
4. Make sure everyone understands each of the options being considered.
5. Choose any two cards and read them aloud.
6. Have the group compare them to each other and choose the better one.
7. Set that card aside; rip the other one in half.
8. Repeat steps 5, 6, and 7 until you have considered all the options and only half of the cards remain.
9. Now choose any two of the remaining options.
10. Read them aloud and have the group compare them to each other and choose the better one.

11. Set that card aside; rip the other one in half.
12. Repeat until you have one and only one card remaining.

For example . . .

▶ The group has eight options. They compare A to B and choose A. They compare C to D and choose D. They compare E to F and choose F. They compare G to H and choose G. This ends Round 1. They set aside A, D, F and G. Next, they compare A to D and choose A. They compare F to G and choose F. Finally, they compare A to F and choose F. Figure 7–6 illustrates this activity.

Tips for success . . .

▶ Have the group first agree what the criteria will be for choosing one option over another. Will it be cost? Ease of implementation? Impact? Some combination of those or other factors?

▶ If you have an odd number of options, make one of the rounds between three cards instead of two. Tear up the two losing cards.

▶ Ripping the losing card in half makes the decision feel more final.

Try these variations . . .

▶ After step 7, compare the winning card with another card. Rip up the loser and compare the winner with yet another card. Continue having the winner take on another option until you have one final winner.

▶ Allow a "holding cell" for options that, if modified, could be real contenders. Do this instead of ripping them up. After the first round of comparisons, visit those options and agree how to modify them before going on to round 2.

▶ Allow each person one "save." When an option that they dearly like is about to be torn in half, they can save that one option for further discussion at the end of the round.

FIGURE 7-6

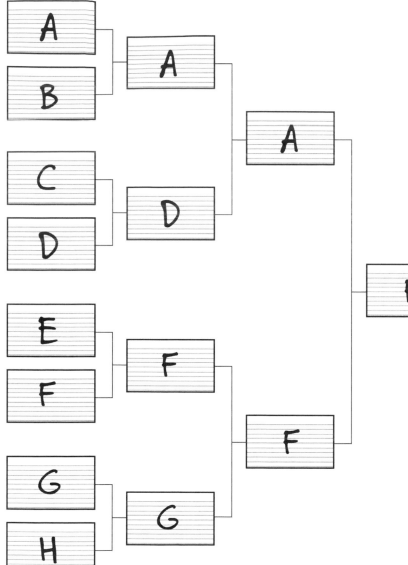

THUMBS-UP CONSENSUS

This is . . .
➤ A prioritization process where participants vote with their thumbs about options from a brainstorming session.

What it does . . .
➤ Helps the group reach consensus after most of the options from a brainstorming session have already been eliminated.
➤ Provides a quick and simple consensus approach that can be done anywhere (no materials needed).

One drawback is . . .
➤ This activity may be too simplistic for a particularly important decision.

What you need . . .
➤ No additional material.

Here's how . . .
1. Review the purpose of the session with the group.
2. Review the results from the brainstorming session.
3. Make sure everyone understands each of the options being considered.
4. Use one of the other prioritizing activities in this chapter to eliminate all but a few of the very best options.
5. Explain how the voting process will now work. A thumbs-up means the participant likes the option and will fully support it. A thumbs-down means the participant doesn't like the option and won't support it. A sideways thumb means the participant doesn't feel strongly one way or another, but would still support it.

6. Call for a thumb vote on the count of three.

7. If all thumbs are up or sideways, the option is selected. Go to Step 20.

8. If there is at least one thumb down, have someone who voted thumbs-down tell why he or she voted that way.

9. Then have one person who voted thumbs-up tell why he or she voted that way.

10. Ask the group if, after hearing both perspectives, there are any modifications that may work for everyone.

11. If there are modifications, apply them, make sure everyone understands this new version of the option, and then go back to step 6.

12. If there are no modifications, vote a second time.

13. If all thumbs are up or sideways, the option is selected. Go to step 20.

14. If there is at least one thumb down, have someone (else, if there is more than one) who voted thumbs-down tell why he or she voted that way.

15. Then have someone else who voted thumbs-up tell why he or she voted that way.

16. Ask the group if, after hearing both perspectives, there are any modifications that may work for everyone.

17. If there are modifications, make sure the modified idea is understood by all, and then go back to step 6.

18. If there are no modifications, vote a third and final time.

19. Regardless of a split vote, the motion carries with a majority. See Figure 7–7 for a flowchart depicting this activity.

20. Plan your action around the selected option.

Tips for success . . .

► Any modification to the original option will change it enough that a new voting process should begin, as preferences may shift in either direction because of that modification.

► With no modifications, there can be as many as three votes. The first two allow for discussion and

(text continues on page 171)

FIGURE 7-7

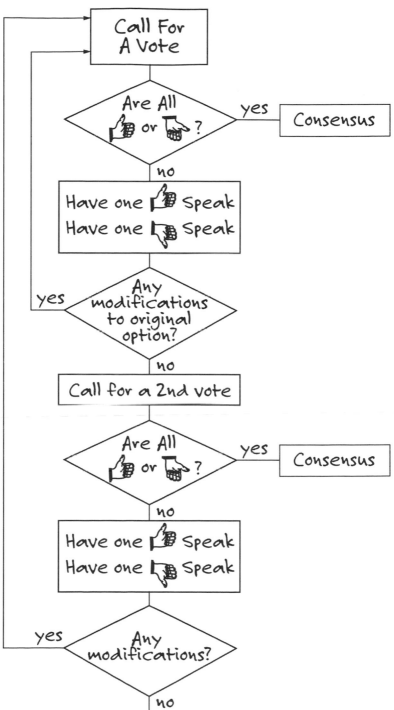

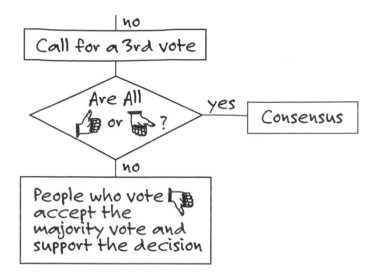

no

Call for a 3rd vote

Are All 👍 or 👎 ?

yes → Consensus

no

People who vote 👎 accept the majority vote and support the decision

modifications afterwards. After the third vote with no modifications, the motion carries with the majority. The dissenting voter(s) concede that their objections have truly been heard and understood, and in the interest of team unity, they will grant their support (or give up on the idea), despite their opposition to the majority position.

► Don't vote until everyone is very clear on the option being considered.

► Define "consensus" for the group before taking the vote. Emphasize that participants don't have to be 100 percent in favor of the option to be able to support it and the team.

Try these variations . . .

► Use up to five fingers instead of a thumb. This allows participants to qualify their support or lack of support. Five fingers mean strongly agree. Four fingers mean agree. Three fingers mean neither agree nor disagree (like the sideways thumb), but will support a majority yes. Two fingers mean disagree. One finger means strongly disagree.

► If after the first vote, the majority have their thumbs down, the option should probably be rejected right then. However, for the sake of those in favor feeling heard and respected, you may still want to go through the rest of the steps. Perhaps those in favor have compelling arguments that will ultimately sway others' opinions.

WEIGHTED SCORES

This is . . .
- A prioritization process where participants assign weights to decision criteria and scores to alternatives in order to determine a mathematically weighted score.

What it does . . .
- Provides a record of the group's thinking process. This is particularly useful when the group's duty is not to decide, but only to recommend.
- Makes the group's decision-making process orderly and visible as they do it.
- Provides a highly disciplined approach to compare options with each other based on agreed-upon decision criteria.

One drawback is . . .
- This activity may be intimidating to some participants (especially when math is introduced).

What you need . . .
- Large writing surface (several flip chart pages posted; large white board; long piece of butcher paper).

Here's how . . .
1. Review the purpose of the session with the group.
2. Review the results from the brainstorming session.
3. Make sure everyone understands each of the options being considered.
4. Draw a large grid. List all the options at the head of each column.
5. Have the group agree to the decision criteria they will use to compare options against each other. List the criteria in the row headings (see Figure 7–8).
6. Have them choose the most important decision cri-

terion and assign it a weight of 10. Have them assign weights to the rest of the decision criteria based on their relative importance as compared to the 10 (see Figure 7–9). Note: There may be more than one 10.

7. For the first decision criterion, compare the options. Select the one that best meets the criterion and give it a score of 10. Score the rest of the options for that decision criterion relative to the 10 (see Figure 7–10).

8. For each remaining decision criterion, compare the options and score as you did in Step 7 (see Figure 7–11). Work horizontally, not vertically.

9. Multiply the weight of each decision criterion by the score for each option to get weighted scores (see Figure 7–12).

10. Total all the weighted scores for each option to get a Total Weighted Score for final comparison (see Figure 7–13).

Tips for success . . .

► This activity works well when there are only a few options to compare. The more options you have, the more complex the process becomes.

► Practice this process before the session. Apply it to a simple, straightforward decision in your own life (where to go on vacation, what car to buy, or the like).

► Consider using this activity after other prioritization activities have yielded a few top alternatives or when the group is having difficulty reaching consensus.

► Because of the complexity of this process, don't use it on decisions that could easily be reached with simpler methods.

► Watch out for some participants who may try to manipulate the system by overloading the weight for a decision criterion that heavily influences their preferred option.

► Do not assign scores for an option in isolation. Always compare it to the other options per each decision criterion. (Work across the grid, not down.)

(text continues on page 180)

FIGURE 7-8

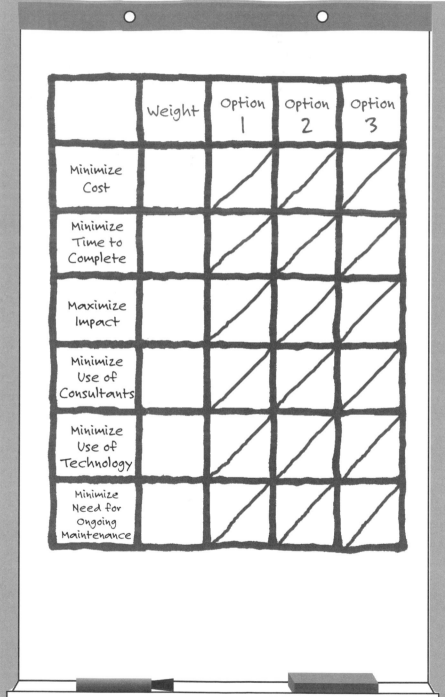

FIGURE 7-9

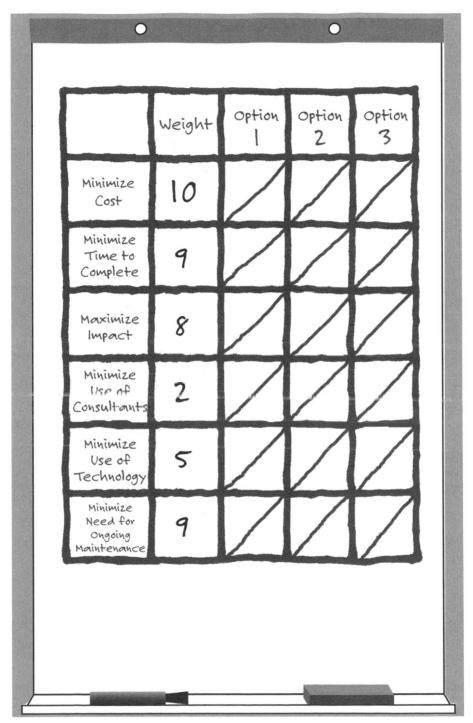

	Weight	Option 1	Option 2	Option 3
Minimize Cost	10			
Minimize Time to Complete	9			
Maximize Impact	8			
Minimize Use of Consultants	2			
Minimize Use of Technology	5			
Minimize Need for Ongoing Maintenance	9			

FIGURE 7-10

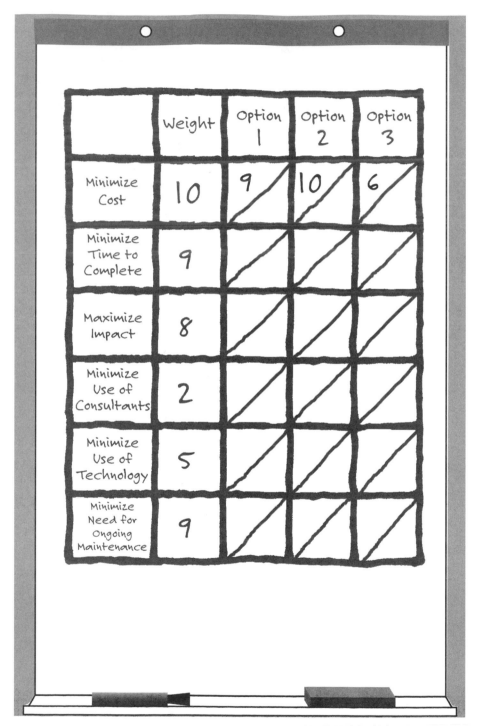

	Weight	Option 1	Option 2	Option 3
Minimize Cost	10	9	10	6
Minimize Time to Complete	9			
Maximize Impact	8			
Minimize Use of Consultants	2			
Minimize Use of Technology	5			
Minimize Need for Ongoing Maintenance	9			

FIGURE 7-11

	Weight	Option 1	Option 2	Option 3
Minimize Cost	10	9	10	6
Minimize Time to Complete	9	10	2	4
Maximize Impact	8	7	7	10
Minimize Use of Consultants	2	7	10	2
Minimize Use of Technology	5	5	3	10
Minimize Need for Ongoing Maintenance	9	6	8	10

FIGURE 7-12

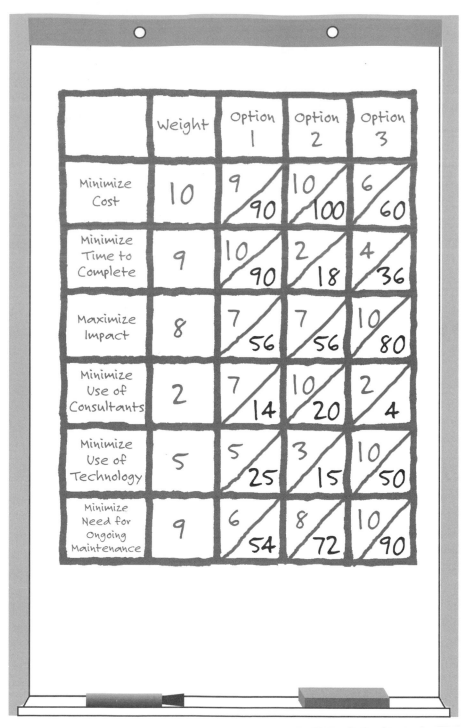

	Weight	Option 1	Option 2	Option 3
Minimize Cost	10	9 / 90	10 / 100	6 / 60
Minimize Time to Complete	9	10 / 90	2 / 18	4 / 36
Maximize Impact	8	7 / 56	7 / 56	10 / 80
Minimize Use of Consultants	2	7 / 14	10 / 20	2 / 4
Minimize Use of Technology	5	5 / 25	3 / 15	10 / 50
Minimize Need for Ongoing Maintenance	9	6 / 54	8 / 72	10 / 90

FIGURE 7-13

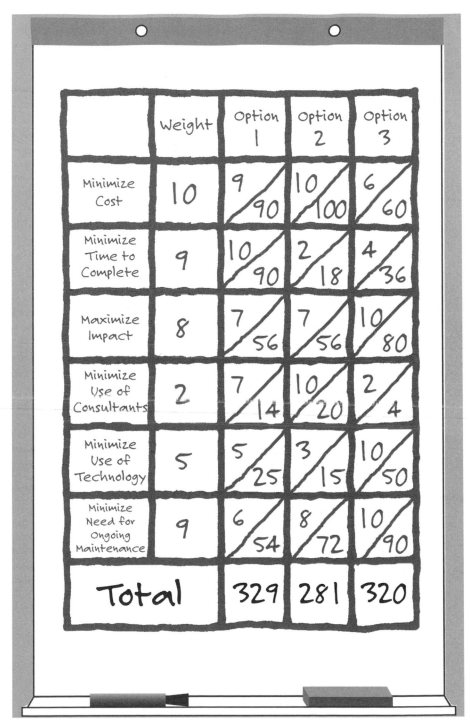

	Weight	Option 1	Option 2	Option 3
Minimize Cost	10	9 / 90	10 / 100	6 / 60
Minimize Time to Complete	9	10 / 90	2 / 18	4 / 36
Maximize Impact	8	7 / 56	7 / 56	10 / 80
Minimize Use of Consultants	2	7 / 14	10 / 20	2 / 4
Minimize Use of Technology	5	5 / 25	3 / 15	10 / 50
Minimize Need for Ongoing Maintenance	9	6 / 54	8 / 72	10 / 90
Total		329	281	320

- Add one more option that represents the "ideal." Consider this as the option that satisfies every decision criterion perfectly. So this option's score will be 10 for every criterion. Comparing the other options to this perfect (albeit fictional) option may help participants see them in a more realistic perspective.

- Add another option that represents your competitor's offering.

- Add another option that represents maintaining the status quo, or doing nothing.

- Conduct this activity in a spreadsheet that is projected for all to see. The math will be done for you (once you program the spreadsheet!). Explore with the group what happens to the Total Weighted Scores when you change the weight of just this or that decision criterion.

- Divide the group into teams and have them all do a step (perhaps step 6? Or step 7?). Then regroup and compare results before moving to the next step.

- Simplify the process by weighting the decision criteria 1, 2, and 3 or other easy numbers. Same for the scores: score 1, 2, or 3 points only.

- Simplify the process by omitting weights. When comparing the options based on each of the decision criteria, just select the one that best satisfies that criterion and give it one point (0 points for the other options). The option with the most points at the end wins.

CHECKLISTS

Checklist for Evaluating a Successful Brainstorming Session

☐ I was very clear on the purpose for the session before I did anything. I knew why we are doing it and what our ultimate goal was for the session.

☐ I invited the right people to the session. This included people who think differently than the majority, or have a different priority about the main topic.

☐ I was conscious of the added power I had in the room as both the boss and the facilitator, and I took steps to neutralize that power.

☐ I selected a brainstorming activity that helped us achieve our stated objective.

☐ I selected a brainstorming activity that complimented our group: our size, our style, and our work preferences.

☐ I crafted a great Focus Question from Chapter 2 that I used to kick off the brainstorming.

☐ I deliberately (and strategically) decided whether to share my Focus Question with the participants before they arrived to the session.

☐ I gathered the materials I needed before the session.

☐ I had the room set up and ready for the participants before they arrived.

☐ I warmed the group up first with an effective icebreaker.

- ☐ I reviewed the session purpose and objective(s) with the group before we brainstormed.

- ☐ I went over the four rules of brainstorming with the group before we brainstormed.

- ☐ I set up the brainstorming activity and got everyone ready to contribute.

- ☐ I asked a great Focus Question without rambling or offering possible responses.

- ☐ I kept the energy high and the pace moving by reacting to their responses appropriately, as outlined in Chapter 2.

- ☐ I recorded their responses per the guidelines in Chapter 3.

- ☐ I helped the group adhere to the four rules of brainstorming.

- ☐ I myself followed the four rules of brainstorming—including the avoidance of positive critiques of participants' input ("great idea," "I like that one," and similar comments).

- ☐ I helped the group process (categorize and/or prioritize) their ideas after the brainstorming was finished.

- ☐ I had the group agree and commit to the next action steps to be taken with the data they had created

Checklist for Creating a Great Focus Question

- ☐ My Focus Question only uses terms and phrases that the participants easily understand.

- ☐ My Focus Question uses acronyms that the participants themselves already use.

- ☐ My Focus Question avoids slang, unfamiliar jargon, or other language the participants wouldn't easily understand.

- ☐ My Focus Question avoids broad, sweeping comments that depersonalize the topic.

- ☐ My Focus Question puts the focus of the topic on the participants themselves.

- ☐ My Focus Question is not so broad and open that it invites participants to address something that is not really up for consideration in the first place.

- ❑ My Focus Question is not so narrow that it limits responses unnecessarily.

- ❑ My Focus Question takes the focus off what has already been decided and puts the focus where the group is truly empowered to make a difference.

- ❑ My Focus Question doesn't lead participants to my answers, nor to answers that someone else thinks they ought to have.

- ❑ My Focus Question leads participants to their own answers.

- ❑ My Focus Question is more than just a bottom-line question—it includes some set-up comments that prepare the participants to respond to that bottom-line question.

- ❑ My Focus Question paints a picture well enough that the participants don't have to exert much effort at all to quickly respond appropriately.

- ❑ My Focus Question ends with a question mark, after which I can stop talking—I won't need to explain it better or elaborate further. It can stand on its own.

- ❑ My Focus Question is so clear that once I've asked it, I don't need to offer the participants any sample responses.

- ❑ I have a different Focus Question prepared for each agenda item of the meeting that will require us to do brainstorming.

Checklist for Keeping the Ideas Flowing Once the Brainstorming Began

- ❑ I actively solicited more responses by using prompts like, "What else?" and "More, please?"

- ❑ I was deliberate when I said "Who else?" and "What else?" versus "Anyone else?" and "Anything else?"

- ❑ I thanked the participants each time one of them gave a response.

- ❑ I refrained from labeling their responses as "good" or "great" or " interesting" or "I like that one!"

- ❑ Unless the activity I used specifically called for it, I refrained from putting people on the spot by calling on them for a response.

- ☐ When in doubt, I paraphrased what I heard to be sure I understood it.

- ☐ I repeated a few of the ideas already given in order to prompt the group to give more.

- ☐ I repeated the entire list of ideas already given in order to encourage the group to build ideas off of the ones they already had.

- ☐ I didn't use either of the above two techniques more than once or twice during the session. (I wasn't too repetitive.)

- ☐ When I saw an obvious idea that they didn't see, I first asked them to consider or look for more ideas in the area that I felt they were missing something (hoping that they would then see the obvious).

- ☐ If they didn't get it from that general question, I offered my idea for their reaction. If they didn't react, I let it go.

- ☐ If they did react positively to my idea, I asked them to expand on the idea.

- ☐ Then I asked them how they wanted me to record it, and I recorded it using their words, not mine.

- ☐ I didn't take credit for my idea later; I let them own it completely.

Checklist for Recording Brainstorming Sessions

- ☐ I used a recording tool and positioned it so everyone could see it.

- ☐ I used a recording tool that I was comfortable and competent using.

- ☐ I used a recording tool that allowed me to transfer our notes to something I could later share with the participants.

- ☐ I used a recording tool that was easy for me to use when I had to edit and otherwise "process" our data.

- ☐ I used a recording tool that permitted us to refer back to our prior work as we moved through the session.

- ☐ I remained close to my recording tool so time (and the group's momentum) wasn't lost with me traveling back and forth.

- ☐ I recorded every idea that was offered—even those that seemed silly or wrong at first.

- ☐ I started recording as soon as they began speaking (so I didn't miss anything), nor did I slow down the group's creativity by making them wait for me to catch up.
- ☐ I recorded everything without making any judgments or criticisms, nor did I give any praise or compliments. I was completely neutral regarding all of their input.
- ☐ I used prompt questions from Chapter 2 as I recorded, to keep the session moving.
- ☐ I recorded their words, not mine; their exact words, not my interpretation.
- ☐ I only recorded the key words necessary to capture their ideas, not every word they said.
- ☐ When a participant got long-winded, I encouraged him or her to summarize their comments, or condense them into a few words that I could then record for them.
- ☐ I didn't allow others to "clean up" or otherwise "fix" a participant's comments—I recorded that participant's own words.
- ☐ Only rarely did I add my own words to the record—and only when I felt I would need them later to help me remember what certain things meant.
- ☐ When I added my own words to the record, I used a different color and/or font and/or parentheses to highlight that those were my words, not theirs.
- ☐ I limited the use of abbreviations.
- ☐ Whenever I used an abbreviation, I spelled it out the first time I recorded it.
- ☐ I only recorded acronyms that all the participants knew and used comfortably, otherwise I spelled everything out.
- ☐ When recording, I used letters that were straight and neat and distinct.
- ☐ I recorded everything large enough so everyone could see it.
- ☐ I used dark colors that were easy to see from a distance, avoiding yellow, orange, pink, and other lighter colors.
- ☐ I used red only to highlight or edit, never as a base color for recording.

- ❏ I didn't try to cram too much onto a page. I spaced my entries so they were easy to read, and so we could edit in between them later.

- ❏ I kept all of their work visible (posted) as we worked through the session.

- ❏ I labeled all charts or pages so it was clear and obvious what information was on each one.

- ❏ I numbered all of the charts or pages so they would be easy to organize later.

INDEX

brainstorming techniques
(*continued*)
  Last One Standing, 50–52
  Mind Maps, 53–55
  Paper Swap, 56–59
  Plus One, 60–62
  Round Robin, 63–66
  Silent Brainstorm, 67–70
  Stickies, 34–35
  Taking Turns, 71–73
  traditional, 32–33
breaks, 9
  when a participant dominates
    the session, 11
  when the group gets stuck, 10
Bubbles technique, 36–42
building on ideas, 3–5

camaraderie, 2
Card Sort grouping method,
  125–127
checklist
  for creating great Focus
    Questions, 182–183
  for evaluating sessions, 181–182
  for keeping ideas flowing,
    183–184
  for recording sessions, 184–186
Chips technique, 43–45
closed questions, 20
colors, for recording ideas, 27, 28
combining ideas, 3–5
competency, in using tools, 25
context of session, setting, 7
creativity, 1, 2
creativity exercises, 75–118
  Associations, 76–78
  Brainstorm Bash, 79–80

Exaggerations, 86–87
Forced Conflict, 88–89
Free Writing, 90–92
Jeopardy, 93–94
Let's Get Physical, 95–96
Mega-Doodles, 81–85
Mind Reader, 97–98
Objects, 99–100
Pictures, 101–103
Reverse Brainstorming, 104–105
Roles, 106–108
Six Perspectives, 109–112
Stop and Start, 113–114
Storytellers, 115–116
Web Surfing, 117–118
critiquing ideas, 3

diversity, 1–2
documenting sessions, 29
dominating, participants who
  are, 11
Dots prioritization process,
  140–143

energy of sessions, 19
environment for brainstorming
  creating, 6
  threatening, 9–10
evaluation
  of ideas, 3, 26
  of sessions, 181–182
evoking responses, 16–17, *see also*
  flow of ideas
Exaggerations exercise, 86–87

facilitator
  editing of participant's
    comments by, 27